D1535464

About the author

My life didn't get off to the best start, but that doesn't mean it has to stay like that. One day I decided I was tired of being unhappy and found the courage to completely change my life and embrace all opportunities that came into my life.

My desire is to help other women who find themselves in similar situations to find their voice and courage to change their lives too, and together we can change the world.

THE RIGHT TO BE ME

Stella Eden

THE RIGHT TO BE ME

Vanguard Press

VANGUARD PAPERBACK

© Copyright 2017
Stella Eden

The right of Stella Eden to be identified as author of
this work has been asserted by her in accordance with the
Copyright, Designs and Patents Act 1988.

All Rights Reserved

No reproduction, copy or transmission of this publication
may be made without written permission.
No paragraph of this publication may be reproduced,
copied or transmitted save with the written permission of the
publisher, or in accordance with the provisions
of the Copyright Act 1956 (as amended).

Any person who commits any unauthorised act in relation to
this publication may be liable to criminal
prosecution and civil claims for damages.

A CIP catalogue record for this title is
available from the British Library.

ISBN 9781784651671

Vanguard Press is an imprint of
Pegasus Elliot MacKenzie Publishers Ltd.
www.pegasuspublishers.com

First Published in 2017

Vanguard Press
Sheraton House Castle Park
Cambridge England

Printed & Bound in Great Britain

Dedication

To Rooster the love of my life, thank you for everything
with all my love.

To live in fear of the past, is not living, it's history repeating
itself.

Acknowledgements

I am fortunate to know some kind helpful people who I would like to thank. Each one of you have helped me in various ways, either with words of advice, acts of bravery, or by being caring in supporting a friend in need, and by helping in my long road to recovery. So thank you to Juliet, Claire & Jim, Maggie & Goff, Annie, Kim, Louise, June, Karen and Diane.

Also I would thank Pegasus Elliot Mackenzie Publishers Ltd for giving me this opportunity to get my story out into the world.

To Chuck and the boys – without any hesitation the wreckage that turned up on your doorstep, you all welcomed me in with open arms into your home, and for all your kindness love and support you gave me, in return you wanted nothing from me, only to be healthy and happy.
Finally to my beloved wonderful beautiful Rooster, you truly are amazing in every way, for all that you do, and all that you have done. There is no one quite like you. I gave you my heart and, in return, you handle it with tender care and love.
To each and every one of you, thank you. With all my love, Stella.

AUTHOR'S NOTE

Each and every one of us enters into a world we have no knowledge of, or of what awaits for us, when we arrive exposed and naked, unable to see clearly with our blurred vision, for our sight has to develop further so we can see clearly the images that surround us. Our ears have yet to become attuned to the different sounds that surround us. Our only way of communicating is through our cries after we have taken our first breath of air into our tiny lungs, as we are unable to communicate or understand the language that is spoken around us. Taken to a location that will be our home, it is here where we will eat, sleep, learn to walk, and talk so that we may communicate, and interact with others. It is through our relationships with our parents or guardians, that we evolve as they shape who we become, in attributing to our character and our beliefs.

By providing a foundation whereby love is unconditional, and the ability to speak freely, encouraged to express all emotions, living in a warm nurturing environment, guided and educated, means we are going to grow, and possibly excel, in all directions in our lives – through the relationships we form, to the careers we choose and the decisions we take upon forming our life experiences. Not having this foundation and being limited whereby our ability to speak, show emotions or express ourselves in any shape or form is prohibited because the consequences will result in you being punished for having them, with no unconditional love, education, guidance or nurturing means you are unlikely to grow, and your options are limited in that you won't reach your full potential.

The relationships we are more than likely to form are unhealthy ones, and often abusive for it is all we have ever known in our entire lives to be treated in this way, it becomes a normal accepted part of daily life, and so we remain hidden and buried away from society.

Yet there are more of us than we know, we are the fourth person standing in the bus queue, a sister, a cousin, a mother, the person who serves you at the checkout till in the supermarket, a next-door neighbour, a nurse, a work colleague, the person walking past you in the street talking to themselves, a photographer, an actress, a singer – we are everywhere in all parts of the world – victims and survivors of abuse. Whether it is emotional, psychological, financial, violent, or sexual abuse, this continuing cycle needs to be broken through educating how unacceptable it is to be this abusive.

Contents

DARKER SHADE OF GREEN

I grew up in a small rural village where there are endless green fields, and a lot of cows, wherever you look there is sure to be a cow in sight. There is one shop, the corner shop we call it. It's a small grocery shop; it sells everything from fruit and vegetables, wooden pegs, to firelighters. If they haven't got what you want, all you have to do is ask the lady behind the counter, and she will get it for you the next day. A butcher's shop, petrol station, garage, school, and a church, that's the entire village. No matter what the time of year, it is always cold due to the easterly wind that blows through the village. It's quite wild at times, even in summer the wind is still ever present. Most of the people that live in the village have very red weather-beaten faces, along with wild eyes, and madness that follows, as the wind sends them a little stir-crazy as it is unrelenting.

With it being a small community everyone knows each other, all the children go to the same school, and every Sunday everyone attends the church service. Nothing is private, everyone knows what is happening in each other's lives. There isn't a great deal of things to do in the village, it is mainly all to do with the church religious activities, harvest festival, jumble sales, bible studies, and the village highlight that they all look forward to is the "Parade walk". Every year the village takes part in this one-day parade to celebrate the village being a Methodist community.

They have numerous lorries, each of them are attached to a long flat trailer, decorated by the women in the village with different coloured material, paper or flowers, and even food, depending what the theme is, which is usually something relating to the bible, farming or the seasons. Amongst the decorations on the lorry, otherwise known as the "float", are the selected children from the village. These special chosen few, dressed in costumes made by their mothers, either standing or sitting on the float waving a small flag with the emblem of the church to the crowds of people lined up on the sides of the roads in the neighbouring villages as the float is driven slowly through. Guided in by the two walking flag bearers who carry the heavy square tapestry flag, adorned with twisted gold rope hanging loosely around each of the wooden poles attached to the flag. It is the male elders of the church who dictate the pace at which the float travels behind them. Banging on the drums announces the start, walking pace, and when other floats from other villages may join in and follow the parade. It is also a cue for them to start singing hymns which continue throughout the parade.

This five-mile round trip finishes with all the floats returning back to where they first joined in the parade, directly outside their church. To continue the parade, celebrations are held at each of the churches, whereby everyone in their village contributes by bringing food and drink. Come rain, hail, sunshine or snow – no matter what the weather, the parade always goes ahead.

Growing up in the village it is better to be a male. Only males are expected to get a job to provide for their family, and to be served by the female, have everything done for them, treat females like dirt. If you are a female you are expected to marry quite early in life to a local red-faced, hairy nostril, dumpy grunting male, have as many babies as possible, chained to the kitchen sink, grow into a narrow-minded judgemental racist gossiping person and never travel further than the village. Why would you want to leave? It has everything a woman could possibly want in life. It's not a woman's place to have a career – she should live there for eternity and die unfulfilled.

I absolutely hated living in the village, and how cruel people living there could be towards each other, because there is so little to do there in the village they get bored, and the main activity beside the church is gossiping, and bitching about each other. When someone is having a bad time in their life, the locals, as they like to be known, thrive off this. It is almost like an addiction to them – they can't stop, and have no desire to for the satisfaction it gives them. The ultimate glory is being the first person to broadcast all the details, along with an added twist, to mark it with their own personal ownership stamp, for this exposure they have on this person or family has to be better than the previous piece of gossip. This constant competitiveness they have towards each grows darker.

Isolation, shunned by everyone in the village, even encouraging their own children to become involved with long periods of silence that can last days, weeks or even months. This is then followed by harassment, whether it be shouting through your letter box or standing in groups of four staring outside your home, or a message chalked on your wall to remind you of your dire situation. If that isn't enough, the intense verbal abuse you will encounter as soon as you step outside your front door is how you will be treated if you or your family are the hot topic of the village.

The best part of the village is the woods because hardly any of the locals would go there, except me. It wasn't that far to walk there, just at the end of the long road that I lived on. I knew them like the back of my hand. I would go there at any opportunity I could, I loved it there. I felt like I was going home, with my Wendy house, blanket, cushion, and jam sandwiches, and a flask of blackcurrant cordial, and my toy chimpanzee monkey. I set up my residency there across the brook, and near the bendy tree. No matter the weather, I was there, with no one to bother me, not even my parents. I would spend all day there eat, sleep, and play to my heart's content. I could be who I wanted to be, have my dreams and aspirations.

GUILTY SEVEN

When I was seven years old my mother decided her life was impossible to carry on living. I remember it was a warm sunny day. I was outside in the back garden, playing pirates on my own. I would pretend that I was trying to escape walking the plank, and needed to hide my treasure. My treasure was a small bag of marbles and a few stones, so I ran into our house to hide it. When I ran into the house I found my mother slumped across the settee in the dining room. Three empty pill bottles on the floor, cigarette still burning in the ashtray and the TV volume on high.

I shook her arm to try and wake her up. I shouted at her, "Mummy, wake up; Mummy, wake up." She just groaned at me, telling me to go away and leave her alone. I ran to a neighbour for help, crying, "Mummy won't wake up." Mother was taken into the hospital and had her stomach pumped. She was admitted to the psychiatric ward for three weeks where she had counselling and electric shock treatment to help her with her nerves. The thought of being given a sedative, a bite guard placed into your mouth to stop you biting into your tongue, and your wrists strapped to the bed while they put a few volts of electricity through your body to help with your nerves just seems too barbaric a treatment to put somebody through. I can't see why it would have helped my mother. It wasn't going to stop my father being abusive to her. It might numb the pain she felt inside. In reality she was going back into the lion's den. But staying with him wasn't going to get any better. When mother was allowed visitors, father, big sister, and I went to the hospital to see her after they had given her the electric shock treatment and counselling.

I didn't recognise the woman at the end of the corridor, standing waiting at the entrance of the ward. It was my mummy. When I realised, I was so happy to see her I ran towards her. As she tried walking towards me she was shaking. Literally, her whole body shook uncontrollably – it was like she was walking on a tight rope, trying not to fall off. Her wrists had these deep black purple bruises around them. She looked like a rabbit in the headlights, so pale, and she had shrunk. My mother is a big cuddly woman but she looked so small. She grabbed hold of me, and hugged me tight like a bear hug – I could hardly breathe. I could feel my mother's sadness and pain, and that she was scared as she clung on to me. From this moment, our relationship changed. She whispered in my ear, "Help me, your father is going to keep me locked in here, he won't let me come home."

I whispered back, "Don't worry, mummy, I will not let that happen." Superhero daughter comes to the rescue and our roles reversed; I became mother to my own mother.

Father shouted and ordered big sister, and I into the dining room. Whenever he summoned us we had to go at once, and stand side by side of each other facing him. If you didn't do this he would spank you with his hand or his slipper. He'd sit down in his armchair in front of sister and me. This was his routine procedure that he always did when one of us had done something wrong that upset him.

Then he would demand to know who did it. Big sister would push me forward, shouting, "She did it, she did it."

The punishment was his black leather belt that he removed from his trousers, and he would pull down my pants, and bend me over his lap – a couple of strikes on my bum cheeks. He always did it just where the elastic in your pants would cup round your bum, so when you pulled your pants back up it would really hurt, and burn when you walked, and sat down. My mind was racing thinking what had we done wrong and I started to panic as I knew what was coming at the end. He told us that he is a great father by looking after us, and that we should be grateful to have a father like him since mother was in hospital, there was no one else to care for us only him. Father's entire family had disowned him. Mother had a brother who worked abroad a lot, and there was only my beautiful grandma but she had the early stages of dementia, and wasn't able to help, and my granddad had died a year ago. Father said that mother had been taken into the hospital, and wasn't well because of us, as we had been bad children, particularly me. It was my fault, playing all the time with my toy train that made too much noise, and I was too loud a child. My train looked like it had been in a crash, the front of it was badly dented, and no sound came from it since father came home from work one day, and found one toy on the floor. This was against his rules – no toys had to be out when he got home from work, no noise from the children, his tea to be on the table, slippers at the side of his armchair. His job could be stressful working in the stationery department for the rail network – very demanding handing out envelopes.

He picked up my train, shouted at mother, and threw it towards me. Luckily, it missed me and hit the wall. My toy train never made a sound again. Father then continued telling big sister and I to look after mother. She has to have rest, and peace and quiet. We needed to do more chores round the house. Most of all, I had to be better behaved, otherwise my actions will make mother ill again, and she will end up back in the hospital. My little heart sank when he said it was my fault. I was so upset I had hurt her. After father's talk I went outside, and sat on the wall at the front of the house. Within seconds I was approached by the reigning queen of village gossip, who lived two doors up from us, appearing from a mist of cigarette smoke, with an all-year-round tan. She hardly ate, and looked like a piece of rotten bark off a tree. She started gently stroking my hair as I tapped my feet on the floor, softly asking me what has happened to my mother. When I just shrugged my shoulders, and continued tapping my feet on the floor her voice immediately changed, becoming aggressive and demanding that I tell her; if not, she was going to report me to the police for trying to shoot her cat with an air rifle. My response infuriated her more when I shook my head to say no. She grabbed hold of my forearm and started squeezing it tighter, and tighter still. I refused to give in to her.

"It's your fault your mother tried to kill herself. It's because of you, you little bitch!"

I just broke down in tears and sobbed. Suddenly, she just let go of my arm and hurried off, mumbling about something burning in her oven. Those words combined with my father's, believing it to be true cemented the guilt inside me.

Father ordered sister and me to go to bed. He said he would come up, and tuck me in bed, and read a bedtime story before I went to sleep. I hated this and I said I would be okay. I even lied to try and stop him. Mummy never does this, I am getting too old, don't like stories, but he was taking no notice. I have never ever felt at ease being with my father. Big sister, and I tried to avoid being in the house alone with him. I can remember from the age of three years old that he gave me the creeps. He would bounce me on his knee then on to his groin. When he got excited he would cough and go bright red in his face. He then would caress my bum. I would pull away from him but he would pull me back, and carry on doing it. I ended up screaming "mummy", and she'd shout at him to put me down. I dreaded bedtime stories with him – he never read me a story. When he came into my bedroom he would sit on the side of my bed, and stroke my legs that were covered up with bed sheets. First the outside of my leg, and then the inside of my leg, whilst doing this telling me that he was a good father, that there are a lot of bad fathers that do terrible things to their daughters and, if I wasn't his daughter, he would fancy me. My heart would beat so fast it was like it was going to jump out of my chest, I just lay there frozen stiff unable to move. My paedophile father was a ticking time bomb waiting to go off. That I should be so grateful, and lucky that he hasn't decided tonight is the night that he is going to sexually abuse me. I started to barricade myself in my bedroom at night. I would drag my chest of drawers, wardrobe, anything to put behind my closed bedroom door so he couldn't get in. I kept wishing that mummy would soon be home from hospital.

My eye has been acting odd, I can see objects in front, and all around me. The difficulty is the position of the images I see. In reality, it's to the right and not to the left; that's how my eye sees it. I am always dropping things, I can't correctly judge the distance to put a cup on the table, and I walk into lamp posts, people and misjudge when to step off the pavements, and I end up with grazed knees from landing on the concreted pavements and roads. Going down the stairs is impossible without falling down them – the only way to prevent myself from falling is to go down each step sitting on my bum.

This lazy eye that I have is being monitored by one of the consultant eye specialists at the hospital. Father has had to take me for my routine appointment with mummy still being in hospital. The consultant eye specialist decided the next course of action is that I should wear an eye patch over my good eye 24/7. This is to make my lazy eye work harder to try and improve my sight in this eye, and to do so for two weeks. When the consultant eye specialist said I would need help, and extra care with getting in and out of the bath, with there being a greater risk of falling as I will be entirely seeing with my not so good eye my heart was pounding. I knew what was coming. It was bad enough at bedtime, I really didn't want him there while I was having a bath. No matter how much I protested to this, the consultant eye specialist sat shaking his head as he looked through my case notes, confirming "your mother states you fall down all the time."

My further plea for big sister to be the one to help me was only to be squashed by father remarking on her inability, and immaturity at being twelve years old, declaring that is what fathers are there for, to look after their precious daughters. My eyes filled up with tears as I stared at the consultant eye specialist, hoping he would notice I was going to cry. He didn't notice I was getting upset and instructed me, "You must do what your father says." Father jumped up from the hospital chair excitedly shook the consultant eye specialist's hand with both hands saying, "I will indeed watch her in the bath."

There was no way out of it but I really didn't want a bath. As soon as we got into the house he immediately went upstairs, and turned the taps on to fill the bath. I shouted for big sister and ran into all of the rooms to see if I could find her hoping she would be in, but she wasn't. Father shouted that the bath was ready. I cried, "Don't want one," but he insisted I was having one. I begged for him to sit outside but he refused, quoting back what the consultant eye specialist had said earlier on, saying "that we had better be quick before big sister came back." He started getting redder, and redder in the face, and coughing. I looked down at the water in the bath. "Get undressed," he shouted at me. I did as I was told, all naked except for an eye patch stuck over my right eye. I stepped into the bath with no help from father; the water barely covered the top of my feet below my ankles. I was about to sit down in the bath, when he ordered I stay standing up in the bath so not to slip. As I stood there shivering cold with my arms wrapped around trying to cover my body, he was insistent, he was going to wash my body.

My refusal to uncover my body, along with my constant pleas that I can wash myself, infuriated him. "You will do as I tell you," and I did because I was scared. I was made to stand in a star position, so that my arms and legs were out stretched and apart, whilst he slowly stroked my body with a face cloth soaked in the bath water, and he proceeded to molest me. He ignores my desperate pleas to stop what he is doing; he needs a little bit longer because he hasn't finished with me yet. When I cry out, "No, I want my mummy," suddenly he just stopped, and dropped the face cloth into the bath water, and ran out of the bathroom. I heard him go quickly down the stairs, and slam the back door. I stood there, naked, cold and trembling. I was crying, trying to get out of the bath. I put my clothes onto to my wet body as quickly as I could. My heart was pounding; I just wanted my mummy. There was no one I felt I could have gone to for help. I just ran out of the house as fast as I could, and headed home to the woods.

SQUARE PEG AND A ROUND HOLE

My Mother struggled being a parent; she wasn't cut out to be a mother. Nurturing, unconditional love and guidance – she didn't have the desire. After mother's suicide attempt I became very protective over her. I became a counsellor to my mother. Every day she would confide in me how she was feeling, and her worries. Mainly about father that he keeps threatening to have her locked up in a mental hospital because she was an unfit housewife. I would reassure her that I would never let that happen, and I could stop it. It never dawned on her that I was only seven years old. I had no power over authority, I am just a kid with a lazy eye that has to wear an eye patch, who walks into lamp posts and falls downstairs because my eye doesn't work so good.

The more emotional and physical support I gave mother, the more she demanded of me, to the point she didn't notice or care how it was impacting on my childhood emotionally and psychologically. My schoolwork was affected – my reading was very poor due to the lack of concentration, all I could think about was is she okay. I worried that she would be trying to kill herself. At break times she would be standing at the gates waiting to see me come out, she desperately needed to talk to me. I had one friend at school; the rest of the kids didn't talk to me because my mother had tried to kill herself. They would taunt me about it. It didn't get any better at dinner time, the queen of the gossip was a dinner lady at the school, and she never gave up trying to get any scrap of information about my mother. Taunting me whenever she had the opportunity. "Your mother not tried killing herself again?"

Going back to the house after school would always end up with big sister, who is five years older than me, physically attacking me. She would scream in a high-pitched shrill to announce her war tune, run up, and charge at me, thump me in the back so hard that she would wind me so I couldn't breathe – this happened daily. Other times she would push me to the floor start punching, biting, slapping, spitting, pulling my hair, nipping, grabbing hold of my arm using both her hands in a twisting action to give me a burn. Before I was born she had all this lovely attention from my grandparents (my mother's parents) then I came along and ruined it all for her. This is why she detests me so much. She started attacking me when I was about six years old, and it carried on until her late teens. While all of this is happening mother's focus of attention is glued to the TV watching her programme. She is oblivious to anything happening in the background, unless it disrupts her enjoyment. Then she can just about manage to shout, without moving from the settee, to "pack it in". To get up and see what was happening requires effort, and time taken away from her precious TV programmes. Then the unwanted attention I receive from father as he returns to the house from work, undressing me with his eyes as he slowly looks up, and down my body.

I would question to myself how I got here, who planted me here? I knew I didn't belong with this family. I hoped, and prayed I was adopted. I was really excited at the thought that I could be, but when I asked mother and she said no, I am their daughter, I was so upset.

Father was back to his usual outbursts of rage throwing anything he could grab hold of against the wall – least little thing, he would flare up and be on mother's case. I found a way to unnerve him. He used mother's mental health against her so many times he was a cruel man, all aimed to control her even more. I decided to use it against him. As he sat at the dining table for his tea, he took a big mouthful of steak pie, chewed and swallowed it. I quietly walked up to him holding my imaginary dog, and pretending to stroke it, and stood there staring at him. He stopped eating and, snapped at me, "Can't you see I am eating?" I whispered quietly to him, "It's funny that meat looks, and smells just like dog food, and mummy is so confused you never know what tin she picks up when I go shopping with her."

He dropped his knife, and fork onto his plate ran upstairs to the bathroom to be sick. When he came back downstairs he looked really pale, and sweat was pouring down his face. Shaking his head, he muttered quietly to himself, "She wouldn't, would she?" He stood staring at mother, she was sitting glued to the TV, chain smoking, unaware of what I had said to him. He never complained about her cooking again. This gave me confidence to stand up to him so I acted even more the weird kid when I was around him by pretending to eat flies, talking to myself, putting piles of grass in front of his armchair. I would act odd in any way I could. It did freak him out, he would shout to mother, "She's acting odd again, do something about her."

Mother couldn't care less; she was pill-popping, eating cakes and chain smoking in front of the TV. It was her way of dealing with it; pretend it's not happening. It stopped him coming into my bedroom.

I was no longer able to go into the woods, which I missed so much. All my time was taken up with helping mother to do the shopping, cleaning, help her with the banking, getting her cigarettes, and extra cakes, and anything else she needed throughout the day. Also she had started at the house making umbrella casings, the metal framework inside an umbrella. A man from a factory would come in a van, and deliver them to your house. The metal rods, and clips are for you to assemble together using a pair of pliers, the more you made the more you got paid. Mother soon got bored of doing them, and it interrupted her watching TV, so I ended up making all of the umbrella casings while she sat smoking in front of the TV watching her usual programmes.

Big sister did whatever she wanted to do, never did any chores or helped with the shopping. She wasn't expected to do anything because, being mother's favourite daughter, nothing was expected from her, and with this golden pass it gave her greater freedom to come and go as she pleased, and she took full advantage. Big sister is a true local girl – she fitted into village life and was very popular with the local dumpy red-faced village boys. They would come and stand outside the house for hours, hoping she would come outside or that they would catch a glimpse of her through one of the house windows.

Whenever I went outside to get mother some cigarettes from the corner shop, they would rush up to me. "Is she coming out?"

"For ten pence, I might be able to find out if she is." I didn't get any pocket money, and nothing from making the umbrella casings. I did quite well out of big sister's popularity. The corner shop sold sweets which were very cheap, so I would buy a bag for eight pence and sell them for twenty-five pence to the dumpy red-faced village boys that were standing pining outside the house, waiting for her to come outside. Big sister did what was expected of a true female local, and became pregnant at the age of eighteen years old. The news travelled fast round the village.

UNDER THE COVER OF ROOF

"You will amount to nothing in life." The words of the school's career advisor assessing my future at the age of sixteen years old. It would be wise to look at getting married, and becoming pregnant is the best I will ever achieve in their opinion. Looking at my grades, a career isn't an option for a girl like me. It is all I have ever wanted – an education and a career. I want more from life than just being stuck living in the village, and expected to live a life that is not for me.

My dream is to become a chiropodist. From the age of six years old, I would go with my parents who went for regular routine chiropody treatment. There at the clinic, where they attended, you were greeted by the friendly receptionist who, after taking your coat to hang on the coat stand, escorted you to sit and wait in the grey comfy chairs until the chiropodist came to call you for your treatment.

I loved the whole experience of going to the clinic and seeing the same chiropodist in their white pristine ironed overcoat, as well as entering the treatment room, that magical world I wanted to be a part of – it was immaculate and so organised. There, waiting for me, my reserved seat positioned at the side of the chiropodist's chair, was a small stool. Laid across it was a neatly folded piece of couch roll to place on my lap, like the chiropodist does during the treatment. Throughout the entire treatment the chiropodist would be constantly explaining to me in great detail what they were doing, and why. They inspired me, and I wanted to become just like them – a chiropodist.

I found it difficult at grammar school – I was bullied a lot, not only in break times but also during classes. Being an androgynous girl wearing glasses I was classed as being weird, and taunted for how I looked, and being ugly. The library was my friend, it was also like a parent in some ways. Through reading the books I found out about starting my period, sex, which knife and fork to use, and some answers to questions I needed answering. Trying to do my homework wasn't easy as mother was forever complaining I was staying up too late doing it, and not spending enough time with her; she needed to talk about her feelings. Father was no better. He had taken his sick depravity to another level, standing completely naked outside my bedroom with an erection. I shout at him for being a sick bastard; he tells me I have a bad attitude, and I am becoming arrogant. Mother couldn't care less and isn't interested when I tell her. Big sister has her own house so at least I don't have to endure any physical attacks from her.

Studying for my exams is more than difficult trying to concentrate, especially when I have to deliver notes to either parent as they are refusing to talk to each other. I wanted so much to do really well in my exams, and two weeks before them and including my final exams mother tried to commit suicide. In total, she tried three times, each time she was found in time, and admitted back into hospital. Somehow I managed to pass all my exams; they weren't the best grades but I did it.

I couldn't afford to go into further education. The nearest college were offering three scholarship places for gifted students who were from poor families. I didn't qualify – I wasn't a gifted student, my exam results weren't the best, the only part I qualify in is that I came from a poor family. My parents were unwilling to help. The money they had set aside in the savings account was only allocated to one daughter, and that daughter was big sister who had no desire to go into further education. The savings went on her entire wedding, and all the furniture, electrical appliances, soft furnishings, carpets, curtains, bedding. You name it, everything was provided for her.

Ignoring the school careers advisor, I enrolled on a youth training scheme, who found me a work placement in a shoe shop selling, and fitting children's shoes. The best part of the job was the training you had to go through before being able to sell, and fit shoes. I loved this as you had to study about all the bones in the feet and how bad-fitting footwear can damage the feet. The pay wasn't great but I was happy not to be stuck inside the house, mother was more than happy as she was able to buy more cigarettes from my monthly contribution paid to her for my board, and lodging at the house. With half my wages taken, it left me with three pounds to live on for the rest of the month.

The chiropodist who had been regularly treating my parents notified them, they would no longer be able to continue to treat them due to retiring from practice. I was saddened knowing I would never see this chiropodist again or be involved in their chiropody treatment.

Details of another practice were passed onto my parents, so they could continue to have their routine chiropody treatment; I just had to go with them. When we got there, the reception area was small and dark, not as welcoming as the previous chiropody clinic. Once you had informed the receptionist you were there for your appointment, you were taken downstairs to the treatment clinic. It was to me like chiropody paradise. My jaw just fell open, I felt like a kid in a sweet shop. I didn't know where to look, there was so much to take in. It was this huge open-plan brightly lit treatment room, with curtains dividing each cubicle, with five chiropodists on either side. I couldn't believe how big it was. Mother's new chiropodists introduced themselves, and asked if I wanted to come in and watch the treatment. I practically ran there, it was so exciting.

A year later, I was still going with my parents to watch them have their routine chiropody treatment done. During one of the visits to the clinic, one of the receptionists came over to me. They had been looking forward to seeing me that day; the clinic had a vacancy for a receptionist and would I be interested? I was so excited, and happy that they thought about me. There was no hesitation from me, I said yes straight away. The following week, I went for an interview and the practice manager explained about the reception work, what was expected of a receptionist working at the clinic. There were also opportunities to further your career if you wanted to at the clinic.

The clinic worked closely with the London faculty training of Chiropody, and they had five scholarships to offer. This entailed a one-year course on anatomy and physiology, followed by entrance exams to sit to see if you qualified for the scholarship. They asked if this would be something that I would be interested in. The practice manager was fully aware of my enthusiasm and avid interest in chiropody, for it is all I have ever wanted to be. A glowing reference from the shoe shop manager secured my position to work as one of the receptionists at the chiropody clinic. My good news wasn't to be celebrated back at the house like I encountered from the warm welcoming happy faces at the chiropody clinic. Instead I was greeted by a physical attack from eight-month heavily pregnant big sister, who was less than happy to know about this achievement I had made. Screaming and demanding to know who the hell do I think I am, and insisting that I am not allowed to do this because who is going to look after mother? With a scrunching rustling noise coming from the empty cigarette packet indicating she needs more cigarettes, snapping at me to go to my bedroom as I shouldn't distress big sister in her condition is mother's only response. So much for my exciting news. I just feel slapped back down and put back on the floor. I know what my sense of worth is; it doesn't weigh much, it never has. Working as a receptionist at the clinic enabled me to buy books on anatomy and physiology so I could attend the course.

I studied hard, and passed the entrance exams, and got the scholarship so I could train to become a chiropodist. With the faculty school being in London I went to live there during my training, much to big sister's annoyance, and she will no longer speak to me. To want to have a further education and a career, she considers me to be a stuck-up, snobby, selfish bitch.

After twenty-three years of marriage, mother felt scared of father and feared for her own safety after he threatened to kill her and bury her in the back garden. Until this point, she maintained she had never been in fear of him. Believing he would want to kill me, she told me not to return to the house because she felt I was at risk, which is laughable. Now is the time to finally acknowledge this danger, and risk only because she felt it for herself. Knowing full well what was happening in front of her own eyes and ears, listening to her own husband talking about fancying his own daughters, her own children, she did nothing about it.

Only then to finally ask me, did he ever touch me. To which I replied, what would you have done if you knew he had? Mother said nothing just sat staring at the blank TV screen, so I answered for her: "you would have done nothing, and stayed with him as you have always done." Two cigarettes were lit, and the TV turned back on, the volume turned up high. She really hurts me by doing this, ignoring what I said makes it worse. Doing this confirms how she feels about me. She really doesn't care; her needs are the most important and no one else matters.

What am I? Just an object in the background? Just use it as and when, and discard it when it's no longer needed? I thought, and part of me hoped, that deep down inside her she loved or cared for me just a little bit, and she couldn't even do that. My value is worth very little – endless cigarettes, cakes and TV. This is what I am worth – hush money offered by the monster and she accepts it.

I did what I have always done and carried on looking after mother, as well as financially supporting her after she left father. I filled all the relevant paperwork for her divorce, attended all the court hearings with her and counselled her more through this traumatic experience. Sadly during this her brother suddenly died, and I had the task of arranging his funeral, as well as consoling mother. He left mother financially very well provided for, to live a comfortable life with enough to have as many cakes and cigarettes as she wanted.

FIVE STEPS

From the hall to the front door it takes just five steps to get out of the house. I never thought these five steps were going to be the hardest steps in my life to take. One man held both my wrists together with his hands, and pulled my wrists up so they were above my head. He held my wrists so tight that my skin underneath his hands were burning, I kept trying to pull my arms down to break free from him. He kept telling me that I am not well, and I have not tried hard enough to be a good wife, I must try harder, and kept saying this over, and over again to me. I begged him to let me go. There was a second man who came over to me whilst I was being restrained. He started shouting in my face, saying I am useless, and a whore, that I am never leaving this house, as it is where I belong, and he could keep me here for as long as he wanted. I was locked inside the house for three hours by these two men. I was eventually allowed one phone call, the second man made the call to a woman. He put the receiver to my ear while I was being restrained. I said to the woman, "You have to help me this is not right." The woman on the phone starts shouting, "Start acting like a married woman, and not a child. Why are you doing this?" and demands to speak to the second man at once. He puts the phone receiver to his ear, and starts nodding his head in agreement with what this woman is saying. My legs are buckling under, I am tired and my arms feel like lead weights. My eyes feel dry inside from crying, there are no more tears. I haven't the energy to carry on. I can't struggle any more.

He turns his head slowly around to face me, and stares at me. In a calm voice, he says to the woman on the phone, "She's mental! Can you hear her? She is hysterical, throwing things around the house! Yes, I know what to do with her."

The man on the phone was my husband, the man restraining me was my father-in-law and the woman on the phone was my mother-in-law.

When Damian said this to his mother, and his father agreed with them, he was still restraining me. I started questioning in my mind. Have I thrown things around, am I hysterical? No, I can't move, and I haven't the energy, and I don't know how to be hysterical. Why are they saying this? Am I going mental? All three of them say I am. No, you are not mental – this isn't right, they are all in this together. The panic sets in. I kept saying to myself that I have to keep calm, you are going to get out, but how was I going to get out? Any chance I could take, I would.

For the fun of it, Damian thought he would try to play strangling me again. He went in deeper with his thumbs this time a lot harder than he has ever done before. My eyes felt like they were going to explode – the pain, not being able to breathe, seeing his eyes staring excitedly as he's doing this to me, pushing and pressing deeper in. I am trying to tell him to stop, and push him off me.

I manage to somehow get him to stop so he let go of me, I rolled off the bed, crawled over to the stairs and pulled myself up. He yelled at me, "You bitch! You hurt me!" I started to cry and I ran down the stairs as he chased after me. As I got to the bottom step so did he, and he pushed me against the wall. I had to get the door keys out from the hall table drawer to unlock the door to get out. I scrambled to get over to the table. He grabbed hold of my arm to pull me away from the drawer, but I manage to pull the drawer open with my other arm and get the keys. He twisted my arm, the pain shot through my shoulder. The keys are in my hand but he is too strong, I can't stop him as he pulls my fingers back to take the keys from me. I sink into a heap on the floor, I can't stop crying. "Cry, you bitch, all you want. I don't care, I have no sympathy for you. I know how to get rid of gutter trash like you."

Damian rips the telephone from the wall socket and throws it against the wall, he walks over and stands towering over me laughing. "No one will come for you, you've got no one, you're pathetic."

I insisted that his parents will help me. Damian decided to put it to the test to see who is right he picked up the telephone plugged it back into the wall, and phoned his parents. Declaring his father is on his way here, he can have me sectioned under the mental health act, all he needed is two other signatures besides his. His parents will back him up, and say that I am mental.

They will do anything he tells them to do because their loyalty lays with him and not with me. If I think it's hell here, then wait till I get in the nut house – you have no rights as a human being, not even able to make one phone call to anyone to get you out. You will be begging me to come and get you released and bring you back home. I sat there thinking, what if he kills me? Will anyone notice or care or miss me? No one knows what is happening or how he treats me – he has totally isolated me.

When I heard the key turn to unlock the front door I got up off the floor, and ran over to Damian's father, asking him to "help me, it's not right how he is treating me." I was shocked, and confused when his father immediately grabbed hold of both my wrists, telling me it would be OK. He looked towards where Damian was standing, and said he came to help him. After one hour of being restrained by my father-in-law he decided he needed to have a rest as his arms were starting to get tired from holding my wrists above my head. He was going to go out for a walk, to give us time together to try and get that loving feeling back into our marriage. I pleaded with him to let me go and that this isn't right. He started to listen to me but then shook his head. "Don't make me choose between you and my son." As soon as he let go of my wrists the redness, and bruising was already starting to show from where he had restrained me. He decided to lock us both inside the house together and take all the keys, refusing to listen to my concerns to leave one set of keys in case there was a fire.

All the windows have at least two internal locks on them. The keys for them are kept locked in his desk in his study. The door to his study is always locked – Damian and his mother are the only ones that have a key to get in to the study. Outside the house the windows have metal bars over them, and there is only one door to get in and out of the house. Once you are in the house, it's hard getting back out. It's like a prison.

Slamming the door shut with the parting words, "If there is a fire, tough! You can both die together," was his father's response before locking the door.

Damian demanded to know why I had tried to leave and why I behaved the way I did, it's not normal the way I reacted. Whenever I was allowed to speak he would interrupt me, and tell me the answer he wanted to hear. He also explained in detail why it was my fault, and where I had gone wrong. For instance he would quote back to me the exact words I had spoken, even when I breathed was included in the evidence he used to prove his point, and make it clear to me that I understood my actions were a clear indication of a lie I had told, or something I had failed to do, and tell him. Whatever I say or do is never going to be right. He had worn me down, there is nothing left inside me. I couldn't carry on any longer. He literally controlled everything in my life – my thoughts, tell me how I felt, what I liked, the clothes I could wear, how to sit, and stand, what food I could eat, how to hold my knife and fork, when to laugh and smile. Even how much sleep I could have and when I could go to bed.

I can hardly speak now there is no point, it's never right. When I do say something, it's his words, not mine that are heard. When I do try, I can hardly get the words out; nothing comes but tears because that's all I have.

"Why, why, why, why, why?" he keeps repeating over and over again like a mantra. I stare back at him with an emotionless blank expression. If I can survive two hours a day of him continually chanting, "You hate me, you hate me, you hate me, you hate me," over and over again in my face. I can get through this. As soon as the front door is opened, I decided,

I am going to run and grab my bag which was tucked under my long coat, hung on the coat stand next to the door – I could see it slightly poking out. Inside my bag were my car keys, purse, and mobile phone. When I get out, get into the car quick and drive away, just go. This is my escape plan. I carried on staring, my heart was pounding, wishing his father would come back soon, and unlock and open the door. What's taking him so long? The sound of metal clashing with a vibration echo I heard outside, it was coming from the gates at the front of the house. His father always flung the gates wide open so they crash, and close together. Not long now, get ready to run! I stood still. I did not want to give my plan away to Damian. I was going to escape. The door handle moved downwards, his father slowly opened the door in case I ran out. He looked surprised I hadn't tried, and that I was standing still in the same spot where he had been restraining me.

He closed the door and walked over to the stairs. I ran towards the door grabbed my bag and opened the door and ran out to my car parked on the road. I couldn't stop shaking, my hands trembling, as I opened my bag and pulled out my car keys, trying to put them in the keyhole in the car door. As I unlocked the car door, I heard the father-in-law shout, "I've found her, Damian, I'll get her." He ran over towards me I dropped the keys on the floor. Frantically, I was looking all over the floor to find them, and I couldn't find them.

"Looking for these?" He stood there, jangling my car keys from his fingers. I looked up saw my keys and started crying. He walked up to me, put his arm around my shoulder. "Come on, love, you're not well. You are in no fit state to be out here on your own, come inside the house with me."

He took me back into the house. I walked in a daze, inside my head was spinning around, feeling like I have just walked out of an aeroplane crash. I couldn't stand straight without wobbling over. His father propped me up against the wall in the hall. Damian stood at the top of the stairs glaring down at me with eyes like thunder, breathing heavily. He was furious with me. "Look at the mess you have made, and what you have put my parents through, what have you got to say for yourself?"

I bowed my head as I had been conditioned by him to do. I have done it so many times, it was almost a natural thing to do when he wants me to speak to him, and look down at the floor because I make him feel physically sick, I am so grotesque, and do what I always do – apologise. Damian asked his father where are his clumsy wife's house, and car keys – he didn't want another embarrassing episode. What will the neighbours think? His father started to check all of his pockets, then pulled his clenched fist from his pocket, and opened his fingers. In the palm of his hand were my keys. I grabbed them both, and ran out of the house, went straight to my car got in, and pressed the door lock down. His father ran out to come and get me, and bring me back again. He was too late. I started the car and drove off. If I hadn't left, I would have been killed by my own hand or Damian's. It was only a matter of time.

THE DUNGEON

It took one year to do up the house, or the dungeon as I call it. It had to be up to his mother's, and Damian's, standards. She couldn't bear it if her beloved son moved into someone else's filth. Filth included anything left by the previous owner – carpets, light fittings, cooker, bathroom suite, even the wallpaper and past decorating. It is all filthy as it has their germs on it; all of it has to be ripped out and replaced. When all the renovations were complete, the new carpets and curtains had to be fitted, and the furniture delivered. We both saved up, his money went towards the deposit for the house, and mine went on all the renovations, and all the carpets, furniture anything what was needed. When it finally came to moving in, I turned up with my one suitcase with all my clothes, and a couple of cardboard boxes. It was exciting to be leaving home, and moving into my new home. Damian had moved in the week before; he had needed time to adjust and settle in.

I knocked on door as it was locked, and waited for him to open the door. He opened the door, his face scowling, and greeted me with "What's that?" looking down into the box I was holding. He was staring at my dragon plant. I had grown it from being a little twig and it was now fully grown. "Get rid of it! I hate it, it looks dirty." He opened the door and I stepped in with all of my belongings. Inside the dungeon, his father was hammering a picture hook into the wall, while his mother held the picture ready to be hung on it. I was surprised to see them both there. His mother quickly came over to me. "Why not leave your things here?" She was pointing to the doormat on the floor.

She decided to give me a tour around the dungeon, and what they had done to help Damian settle in. On all of the walls hung Damian's pictures – he had a vast collection of religious paintings all to do with being catholic, a crucifix in each room. His mother was very excited, and very keen to take me into the lounge, her favourite room in the entire house, to show me this wonderful picture I must see. There, hung above the fireplace, a photo in a large imposing gold affect frame of Damian as a baby being nursed by his mother, whilst she looks down lovingly gazing at her son. You couldn't help but notice it as soon as you walked into the room, it was slap bang in your face. It was a nice photo, but I didn't feel it should be there and thought it was odd. Damian shouted to his mother to come in here to look, and see what she thought of the position of his clock in the dining room. I followed her through, whilst they were both deciding where it looked the best. I looked around the room and noticed all of his personal items, books, ornaments, and more photos of his mother all put in their rightful place on show. There is no space for anything else to be put there. Damian's belongings filled the entire dungeon, he had so much stuff it was full to popping. When he moved in, he marked his territory in the dungeon by taking as much space as he wanted. It wasn't enough for him that he had his own double bedroom, and a large study, the entire basement room that ran underneath the lounge and dining room, he needed all of this space as well. When I moved in the only place for my belongings was to be put in my bedroom, and nowhere else. It is non-negotiable.

All the furniture had even been placed in exactly the same position as it was in his parent's house. Even in all of the cupboards, and drawers in the kitchen, the plates, cutlery, pots and pans, everything was identically placed inside them. His mother took me to one side, and touched my arm. "Word of advice, my dear." Your time will never be your own, he gets a bit irritable. Take no notice, it will pass; he easily gets a bit homesick." Shouted to her husband to bring her coat, and take her home, kissed her son on the cheek goodbye and said they would be back on Monday to collect his laundry. Damian gave them a key he had cut for them, so they could come in whenever they wanted to. The door was closed and locked straight away, then he turned around and smiled. "There are a few things we should discuss about living together, get all the potentially embarrassing things out of the way, then it's better for everyone."

The dungeon has to be cleaned daily, due to his dust allergy. He isn't very talkative in the morning, likes it to be quiet, otherwise he gets a bad head and can't focus at work – he needs to be on the ball, being a solicitor. The last person to leave the house has to check that everything is switched off, and the dungeon is locked secure. Was there anything I needed to tell him about me? There wasn't anything else to tell him about me. Damian forgot to tell me a lot of other things about himself. He started very slowly manipulating, adding more to his rules, and becoming more controlling. I didn't realise what he was doing to me.

He decided after two weeks of living in the dungeon that it wasn't secure enough – we needed more locks on all of the windows, so his father came and fitted two locks to each window. But this wasn't good enough. He had seen an advert in the local paper, metal grills that fitted onto the walls, and covered the entire window, you would have to be a snake to get through the metal bars. He had them fitted on all of the windows downstairs. One weekend he counted at least four people walking past with their dogs all staring at the dungeon with the metal grills over the windows. From now on, all the curtains have to be kept closed, never opened, as he is convinced they are all potential burglars. One day when he arrived home from work he was interrupted by a rude man, who knocked on the door, trying to sell dusters. The day after, I got home from work and found he had put a massive padlock on the gates to stop anyone coming on to his premises. He peers through the curtains, and sees me standing at the gates, comes to unlock the padlock so I can get into the dungeon, then clicks the padlock to lock.

Once inside the dungeon he demanded to know, "can you explain why?" and pointed to the empty plug socket. The switch was up, indicating it was on. I had checked all around the house this morning to see if the lights were off and they were, so I locked the door and went to work. He started pacing up and down in front of me, snorting as he breathed, glaring at me. "Do you realise you nearly caused a fire and we could have lost the entire house?"

All I could say was, "I am sorry, I didn't mean to leave it on. I am sure it was off, I must have missed it this morning. The house is OK."

"Missed it! How can you? It's next to the bloody door! Are you thick? I won't stand for this attitude! I have had to sit over it until it has cooled down in case it ignited, because you're too lazy to turn it off."

I kept apologising, I wasn't sure whether it was on or off before I left for work. Damian wouldn't let me move from the spot where I stood. He was pacing back and forth in front of me, wanting to know why I let it happen, how could I have let it happen. Whatever I said he kept turning it around then I got so confused, I was getting tired, and I felt sick. I was hungry as I had not had anything to eat since lunch. After an hour, he decided to forgive me, but I must never ever let it happen again, and to make certain that I didn't do this again so I could be trusted, he demanded that I had to show him what safety checks I do before leaving in the morning, and to go through each room there and then, and physically show him. My five-minute house check has now turned into an hour's safety check, which he shows me then in turn I have to do this in front of him the exact way he does it. All the lights are switched off, each bulb has to be physically touched including ceiling lights to see if they are cold, not hot, even if the light hasn't been used this must still be done.

Any plugs in the sockets are to be unplugged, and the switch on the plug is to be switched off. Then using the back of your hand to touch it to see if it is hot, and then using the palm of your hand to check it again. All the windows need to be checked that they are locked, and after make sure there are no gaps between the closed vertical blinds as it lets sunlight in, and people will be able to see through the gap into the house. Stare at the turned off lights for five minutes to make sure no sparks of electric are getting through. If the bulb is hot, wait until it has cooled down and re-check it. Feel around both fireplaces to make sure they are turned off, sniff for gas, and the same around the cooker. Check all the taps are off, and the water supply is turned off under the sink. The safety checks are to be repeated five times in each room and, once this is completed, the door to the room is to be closed. Only when it has all been checked can you then leave the dungeon. When the front door is locked, make sure there are no gaps around the door seal, and the door fits snugly. Then try the door handle five times to make sure it is locked, and finally put the padlock on the gate, and check this is locked again five times. And finally off to work. This is to be done when leaving the house, even when I have to go to the dustbin or into the garden.

"You dirty bitch, look what I have found." I couldn't see as my eyes hadn't adjusted to the bright ceiling light beaming into my bedroom. I put my arm over my eyes, trying to see what he had. I rolled over in my bed looking at my electric alarm clock in red numbers four thirty a.m.

I turned to see Damian pressing his thumb, and forefinger together but still I couldn't see anything. He shouted, "It's your bloody hair! Well, don't just lay there in bed, you better get downstairs, and look at the cooker, it's filthy, full of your dirt."

I dragged myself out of bed and went downstairs to the kitchen. There stood Damian bending over the cooker, pointing to the evidence with a pen. It was one strand of my hair laid across one of the control knobs. Another strand of my hair he had placed on a piece of kitchen paper, this was the offending single strand he was holding between his thumb, and finger in my bedroom. He had decided to get up earlier to get ready for work when he went into the kitchen for breakfast, and saw this. It made him vomit, now he feels terrible – his stomach is in agony, he doesn't know how he will cope with his case load today, and the court hearing he has to attend. How could I do this to him, knowing full well he had this important case? If he wins, it will be ground breaking; it will allow other solicitors to sue the police for their incompetence, no other case like this has ever been successful. What have I to say for myself this morning? Making him ill and trying to deliberately sabotage today of all days – why have you got to ruin it? I apologised.

"Sorry! You are always fucking sorry, it's not good enough! You always spoil things for others, with that twisted sick mind you have. You never want anyone to be happy. You're mental, just like your mother; it's all about you."

He flung open the cupboard door under the sink, and pulled out the cleaning box that has all of the kitchen cleaning products, and pushed hard into my chest. I stumbled backwards into the wall. He told me to get on with cleaning my mess – he would be checking to see if I had done it properly when he returned home after work. He slammed the front door, and left for work. I cleaned the cooker, and did the security checks, and went to work. I worried all that day that he might not win, and with him being sick because of my hair. When I returned back after work, I unlocked the dungeon door, and slowly opened it. I was greeted with a very happy smiling

Damian – he had won the case, and commented that the cooker looked great. He had got me a present which he had the young woman in the store gift wrap for me. He hoped I would like it and said that I should open it carefully so as not to damage it. I was quite excited wondering what it could be. There, laid on my lap, was an A5 black leather-bound lined five hundred cream-paged notebook, and silver-looking pen. He thought it might be useful for me to have. That weekend Damian had a list of errands he wanted doing but he simply hasn't the time to do them, what with work being so chaotic – would I mind doing them? He wouldn't normally ask but he really needed these items getting. I agreed to help him.

"You might want to write this down." He walked over to where I was sitting, and handed me the leather-bound notebook and pen.

Delusional Demi-God

Damian was born with a silver spoon in his mouth, I kid you not. When he was born, within minutes his very wealthy grandfather went to the hospital, smoking a big fat cigar to see his new grandson. He pulled out from his inside jacket pocket a silver spoon, and put it in Damian's mouth declaring, "My grandson will want for nothing, he will have it all."

To listen to Damian telling you about his childhood, where his mother would spend hours painting pictures with him, doing various activities together, and the long walks in the parks where she taught him all about the wildlife, and the trees, and what they are called. The wonderful sunny family holidays at the seaside, staying for a month at least three times a year in the cosy whitewood cottage that they rented, situated within walking distance to the beach. It has glorious views overlooking the cliff tops, to see the sea, watching the fishermen trawling for fish in their small boats. His father didn't stay at the cottage, although he longed to be there with his wife and son. He owned a small grocery shop, and couldn't take time off as he did everything in it from serving customers, stacking shelves, collecting the groceries, and selling them in the shop; he was a one-man band. Damian and his mother had a great time together on the beach going crabbing, collecting shells, fetching firewood for the fire.

It sounded a perfect childhood, and very idyllic in every way. But in reality this was the furthest away from the actual truth. His mother was an overbearing control freak, trying desperately to have total control over her husband, she was in a battle fighting against her mother-in-law. She was envious, and wanted the lavish lifestyle that her mother-in-law has. Beautiful handmade clothes, shoes, anything she desired she got it. The mother-in-law thought her daughter-in-law wasn't good enough for her son, and that she is just a gold digger from a poor family who was just after the family business, and the money. Personality wise they clashed over everything – which catholic school Damian was going to attend, how the grocery shop should be run, even to the opening times. Whenever they met, it often ended in a heated argument. They would turn to face Damian's father, and both stare at him as if to say which one of us is right. This put pressure on him, for they both demanded to know which side was he going to take – his wife's or his mother's side. Either way, he wasn't going to win with these two women – they both wanted his total loyalty, but it could only be to one of them.

His way of dealing with it was through anger, and alcohol. A man of very few words, with the rage burning inside him, he would express himself by shouting in a blind drunken fury, attacking the furniture, and smashing up the contents in the house with his fists, going through it like a whirlwind, destroying all that comes in his path in front of his wife and son. Over the years he became an alcoholic and drank away all the money from the business, and all of the savings until nothing was left. Damian's mother resented her husband, she was back to living the poor life. Before she met Damian's father she had a brief job in her life, as a cook's assistant to a wealthy family that imported manufactured steel. This opened her eyes to what wealth could bring, and the doors it could open. The respectability this family had in the community all through wealth, this is what she wanted – she had a taste of the good life. There was no way she was going back to work again – her role was mother to Damian. She has to be there for him and his needs. Their gleaming new leather interior family estate car had been traded in for a rusty white van with cigarette burns in the seats, and the driver's side window that got stuck when you wind it down. To close it, you had to pull the window back up with your hands. Inside the van on either side were shelves, and a small counter that went across the depth of the van.

With the remaining money from the sale of the car they bought fruit, vegetables and tinned goods, just like it was in the grocery shop. Except now his father would drive round the streets, and park his van, and shout out in his booming voice "Grocery man," open the rear van doors, and trade from his van with a half-empty bottle of whiskey in the front of the van. Damian deeply hates his father for what he has done to his mother – his love and loyalty went only to his mother. He has this deep connection with his mother – they are on the same wavelength with this unbreakable bond that exists just between the two of them. He talks to her every day for hours about anything from politics to religion. She is totally devoted, and idolises him. He can do no wrong in her eyes. His father struggles to have a relationship with him, but Damian is defiant. He is determined never to have a relationship with his father. Damian feels his father needs to be punished, and reminded of what his failings are. He would instigate arguments with his father, and just keeps pushing on his father's anger button a little bit more where it would go. It resulted in them fighting, and Damian ended up with a cut on his cheek due to being pushed through a glass window. After the fight Damian started to experience headaches, which the doctor said was stress due to exams, unaware of what had happened.

It is essential to his mother that no one knows in the outside world what is happening in their messed-up, dysfunctional family life. They would portray themselves as a plain family that went regularly to church, and had a successful grocery business. What happens behind closed doors stays there. The doctor said the headaches would pass but, just to help him through it, prescribed soluble pain relief. After the exams, the headaches were getting worse, not better. Due to his age, the doctor was reluctant to give Damian anything stronger. His mother was taking prescribed high-strength pain relief as she had started to have health problems all brought on by the stress caused by her husband, and her mother-in-law. She gave Damian some of these tablets, which stopped his headaches. He continued to take the full dose as instructed by his mother, every day for five years. By the time he was eighteen years old, he was addicted to them. The tablets that had relieved his headaches had stopped working, and now they were starting to affect his sleep due to the pain in his head. He didn't get more than four hours sleep and on some nights he had none at all. Stomach cramps, and constipation followed. He would regularly overdose with the pills, popping them in his mouth like they were sweets to try and stop the pain in his head, but not even this worked – the pain was getting worse. He eventually went to see the doctor who prescribed him the highest strength in this level of pain relief, a lot stronger than his mother's medication.

If this didn't work, the next pain relief would be a morphine-based tablet. The new tablets worked for a while. During the sleepless nights that Damian laid awake it gave him time to think about the conversations he has had that day. Like a game of chess, if he moves his knight, what does that make his opponent do? What is the outcome? Who will it favour, him or the opponent? The final result always has to be the same – he wins because he is the superior one. Night after night Damian refuses to allow himself to sleep. He keeps awake by reading law books, learning them, reciting them almost like a chant – word for word, over and over again, repeatedly going over past events in his life, dissecting each and every moment. Sleeping is a weakness like his father who needs eight hours. He will not allow himself to become weak. Mistakes are a weakness. Damian is never wrong about anything, he never makes any mistakes so therefore has never had to apologise for anything in his entire life because he is never wrong. Verbally he has to prove his point – that he is a superior person to you. With his intellectual legal mind using his extensive vocabulary, he always has to have the last word during a conversation, because he decides when that conversation ends. Whatever you say during a conversation to him he will accept that is your belief, it's set in stone – you have exchanged a verbal contract with him.

This cannot be rectified even if you change your mind or decision – you only have one chance. There are no second chances, you failed. Victories are all about the winning, to satisfy himself that he is the better person. If he can't get under your skin or put obstacles in your way to make it difficult for you, he will mark you with a bruise from his punch.

Damian likes the communist regime where people are told what the rules are for living and they must abide by them – if they don't, as a result they will be punished. It would be far better for countries to adhere to this, or to be run on a more military basis. He likes the discipline, and the routines they install in their daily lives so everything runs smooth in an orderly manner. Nothing interrupts Damian's routines – everything has to work around them. The alarm clock is set at the same time each day. Everything in his life has a procedure, each has its own set routine, and allocated time slots from going to bed, to waking up on a morning, getting dressed for work, when to have meals, cleaning teeth, going to the toilet, workout in the gym, even to how long he spends in the bath. Weekends have a set routine too. Time is taken up with his activities – TV, reading, watching DVDs, and any spare time there is has already been allocated to another routine or event due to his planning. Nothing can be done on impulse, it all has to be planned weeks ahead, even just going to the cinema or to see a friend.

Not that he has many friends; he has just one friend that he sees twice a year. He feels sorry for the poor chap as he has no prospects in life – he is a bit of a loser whom he worked with at a legal firm, and out of the goodness of his heart he can spare him four hours of his time and offer him a piece of cake a hot drink, and tell him where he is failing in life. Damian has no tact, he just says what is in his head. If you find it offensive, he really doesn't care; he has no compassion and lacks any understanding of anyone's situation in life. For he has suffered and had the worst life anyone could possibly have. Failed by his parents for not having the funds to send him away to university to study law, instead he had to make do with home study for the same qualification degree, and because of this all the law firms look down on him, and it has held him back in his career. Not that his own actions at the law firm where he worked at had anything to do with his failing career. Planning a war against one of the partners because he felt like it. His main grudge against him was he didn't like the look of him, and that he was a snobby bastard who went to university and was given the partnership job at the firm by Daddy, who owns the law firm. He could slit his throat because of how he acts, so full of confidence in front of everyone who works there. So he bases his plan of attack on the pretence of a pay rise, whether he gets one or not he doesn't care, he received a generous one eight months ago.

The main aim is to make this man's life difficult, and to cause him to suffer. This resulted in the firm hiring a man whose sole job was to try and resolve this situation they had with Damian. During the board meeting Damian had with the partners of the firm, he had hidden inside his jacket pocket a Dictaphone to record the conversation. He had prepared a list of questions, and rehearsed them through the night, to get them to give him the answers he wanted. So when he played back the tape recording of the meeting, he would edit parts of it to erase parts of the conversation. The end result was the partner's voices on the tape recording saying exactly what he wanted them to, admitting they were at fault and they had breached his contract. The new man was brought in to investigate, and to find out what Damian's evidence was, and what he proposed to do. All of his findings were to be reported to the board of the firm on a daily basis. The board members were putting pressure on this man to get it sorted. Damian upped his game to cause mental pressure by harassing this man. Bombarding him by sending him excessive numbers of emails every day, following him from his car into work, sitting outside his office six or seven times a day, even after work standing outside in the dark waiting by this man's car to tell him all of his unreasonable demands, deadlines for answers or he will sue under section whatever, and reveal his evidence to the judge, not to mention the newspapers. This went on for two years.

The end result of this war was the hired man ended up being signed off on long-term sick leave due to stress all brought on by Damian. He never got the pay rise nor did the firm recognise any of his hard work at winning court cases. It highlighted that he was trouble and very difficult. Probably it alarmed them what extreme lengths he would go to. Three months later everyone who worked at the firm received a letter including the cleaners, stating the firm was restructuring the job titles, and roles. Some jobs were at risk of the hours being reduced. Damian was the only one in the firm whose position was affected. They could no longer offer him his current position where he attended court hearings, dealing with clients and swearing affidavits for the court. He was offered a position of chasing debt payment from the insurers for any outstanding balances owing to the law firm, for the work they have done for the insurers. Working two days a week on his current full-time wage was the offer that they put forward to him. Due to the restructure, they would completely understand if he decided to seek employment at another law firm, and would appreciate a written response from him in two weeks' time whether he accepts or declines their generous offer. They were unable to fire him due to the employment laws, as he had pointed out that were in his favour. He couldn't take them to court and sue them because the new position and salary being paid is excessive for what is part-time work.

It would have been thrown out of court as the whole war was planned, and based upon a pay increase. The ammunition he got to have control over them was worth nothing. During the two weeks, he contacted three law firms – these were the only ones in the region where he works who practice in his type of legal work. Damian will not work out of the region as it would result in a house move. This is never going to happen – he would be too far away from his beloved mother. He made an appointment to see each secretary, to deliver in person his CV for the partners at each firm to view, in the hope they would consider giving him an interview. Each one of them humbly greeted him and appreciated that he had taken the time to visit their firm in person. They apologised for the inconvenience as they needed to take his CV into another room and to make a brief phone call. The frosty response after this brief phone call, from all of the secretaries, was not what he was expecting to receive. They all repeated back to Damian with an abrupt, "No, we cannot accept your CV," and handed it back to him with no explanation. He scurried out like a belittled rat – nowhere to go, no one wants him. According to him the law firm had screwed him big time, he couldn't get another job as they had him blacklisted with all the law firms. He might as well kill himself, there is no point in living. They have ruined his life. Why him, why not someone else? It's not fair, he doesn't deserve to be treated like this.

If Damian did attempt to kill himself, his mother had her own plans; it involved a gun aimed at the senior partner's head. He loves the thought of his mother willing to sacrifice everything for him and her ultimate dedication towards him. It is what he expects of her. To save his mother from a future life behind bars, and the scandal in the newspapers for her, he has accepted the offer of the new position at the law firm. According to his calculation, he isn't really working two days a week. It is more he does an eighteen-hour shift on a Monday and the same again on a Tuesday; in total thirty-six hours, which qualifies as full-time. The opening hours of the law firm are Monday to Friday nine a.m. to five-thirty p.m. The earliest time any person working there can be in the building is 8:30am. The building has to be vacant by five forty-five p.m., this is when it is locked and patrolled by the security guards at night, due to various attempted break-ins mainly for the computers. His mother is happy he is working less especially when it is cold and dark outside as he should be indoors keeping warm as he might get a chill on his chest. She worries constantly that when he is travelling to work on the trains, someone might be lurking around a corner to attack him. Unlike his mother, Damian fears nothing, as fear is to be weak. He regularly goes to a boxing club has done since he was a child to help control his aggression. His mother has never forgiven the old family doctor for implying that her son was holding in emotions possibly due to abuse by them.

At a young age he was displaying the same behaviour like his father when he smashed his way through the house. His mother said the doctor had bribed him with a toy to say they were mistreating him. All he needed was exercise to get the aggression out of his system. Being punched in the face gives him a buzz; he craves it, he likes the pain, and how it makes him feel. After a while this pain wasn't enough, not like when he cuts himself with a razor blade. He is the one in control – when to cut and where.

Running On Empty

Within a year of living in the dungeon, Damian's rage would erupt several times a day, a bit like a ticking time bomb. You're just waiting for it to go off, the slightest wrong movement or noise, just my presence being in the same room as him could be the trigger. The physical destruction he causes inside the dungeon includes smashing furniture against the walls, even punching the walls, and kicking the doors so much that at the end of the attack they are barely hanging on to one of the hinges. He is like a tornado, anything that comes in his path gets destroyed during his violent outbursts. It isn't his fault the way he acts, it is entirely all my fault; I am the one who is responsible due to my bad behaviour that has caused him to act this way. For standing incorrectly, giving him a pen with no ink in to write with, his shoes not cleaned properly, for speaking too loud, too quiet or breathing wrong – all done with malicious intent to ruin his life. He feels it is important that I am there to witness the pain I cause him, and to see his blood splattered on the walls where he repeatedly punches them, shouting out my name every time he punches into the wall. I stand in terror frozen to the spot. Afterwards he walks over to me, and starts circling around me like a wolf ready to pounce on its prey, telling me how worthless I am. He knows about my fucking sick mind games, I am playing with him, he is on to me. I try telling him I don't mean to upset him. No matter what I say, it's never right. All I can say is I am sorry. "Can you explain to me why?" This is always the start of his interrogation; I feel like I am in court in a witness box being tried for a crime I didn't commit.

You can't reason with him, he has got all the answers. He decided, during another night of insomnia, what tomorrow's war against me will be. He has it all planned out – when to start his interrogation to when it ends that day, it can last between two to four hours or all day, it depends on how many of my failings that he feels he needs an explanation for. It used to be once a week, now he is shouting at me every day. He can justify the interrogations are necessary because he has evidence about my failings through recent or past conversations he has had with me. He often tapes the conversations, and plays it back to me over and over again. He dissects each word, and notes how I stood during the conversation, my body language, when I breathed, how my facial expression was, and my eye movements. He wants to know why I behaved the way I did at these points during the conversation – do I know the distress it causes him, my continual selfishness? When he dismisses me after the interrogation you think he is all done. It's just the beginning to the next level. As I leave the room he follows me, and walks so close behind me that he is tripping over me. His toes are hitting the back of my heel –it's almost like he is like a leech glued on to me. He starts to chant, like a mantra, "you hate me, you hate me" over and over again; this can last an hour until his voice gets a little tired, so he pauses for a few minutes and starts over again. I frustrate him by showing no response.

61

"I can make you hate me! You are so fucking stiff, you are no fun, I am bored! Make me laugh!" He comes over and pinches the skin on my arms but this doesn't amuse him enough. When he crosses his arms to put my head into a wrestling head lock, this makes him laugh, even more when I cry out in pain. He knows where my selfishness towards him comes from – it's all from having too much sleep. To stop me going on a downward spiral, heaven knows where it will lead me – probably glue sniffing on a park bench with all the smack heads shooting up on heroin. To save me from myself he decides to reduce the number of hours I sleep. I can't go to bed until he is ready. Each night he stays up that little bit longer than he did the night before. At eleven p.m. he turns off the TV then gets up from his armchair, and walks over to the door. At this point I have to get up to follow him upstairs. He proceeds to walk through into the hall, and he pauses for five minutes at the bottom step of the staircase, and stares looking up at the crucifix hanging on the wall at the top of the staircase. I am never allowed to be in front of him when walking, always three steps behind. He requires complete and utter silence – this makes him more connected to his Lord Almighty. I made an error by walking out of step – when he stops, I must stop at the exact time, never a step ahead, which I did and stepped on the creaking floor board. My eyes hadn't fully adjusted to being completely in the dark – no lights are ever to be switched on, they are too bright for Damian's sensitive eyes. The glare of the light coming from the switched on TV is the only light allowed on in the dungeon.

My ultimate act of selfishness is damning god as he was blessing Damian. "You just couldn't be bothered," he mutters through his sticky cloggy nasal canal, breathing down the back of my neck as he says it. "You better get on your knees, and pray for forgiveness for stepping into the devil's path, you are the fucking whore of Babylon! You are going to burn one day for your sins and I won't help you. I will just stand and watch you, listening to you screaming out in agony for help, but it will be too late for you, the Devil will take your soul! You, don't you believe me, you know I am always right. Now we have to stay up so I can reconnect with the Lord Almighty, I could be all night waiting for the sign." My knees are numb from the pain. I tried sitting back on my feet to take pressure of them, it didn't help. I need to get up and move my legs. At midnight Damian has been blessed by the Lord Almighty, after which he takes in a deep in breath of air, puffs out his chest, and beats his chest, declaring "know who I am." He starts to go up the stairs – the third step gap applies even to walking upstairs behind him. His mother worries her son will fall down them and I am there to cushion his fall in the event of it ever happening, especially when he stretches up to kiss the crucifix on the wall at the top of the staircase. Then goes into the bathroom to brush his teeth. I have to be ready with my leather-bound notebook and pen, waiting quietly in my room – he doesn't like to be kept waiting after he has said his prayers in his bedroom. When he is ready he shouts my name to indicate he is ready to be addressed. I have to knock three times on his closed bedroom door, and wait for him to call enter.

There is an area where it is acceptable for me to stand – straight, not slovenly; three steps from the bedroom door. If I stand further from this point it strains the back of his neck. Damian sits upright in bed and laid across his body are the bed sheets ironed pristinely by his mother with not a crease in sight. This is when he informs me what errands that he needs doing. Every night I have to write them down – there can be at least sixty to a hundred to be done by the end of the week. Each errand that I have completed has to be marked with a tick at the side of it, with the date and time marked next to it in the notebook. All phone calls I make on behalf of him, I have to write a log to record the date, time and the name of the person I spoke to. The exact wording of the entire conversation has to be written down, and handed over to him for him to read.

Go into the doctors, never phone them, to order a repeat prescription as they won't do it, go back there two days later to pick it up. Don't go to the chemist across the road from the doctors to have it dispensed – the pharmacist tampers with the tablets, can't be trusted, so go to the one fifteen miles away; they have a trustworthy pharmacist, according to his mother. Suits need dry cleaning, they need to be back in three days' time; take them back, they are not clean enough. New DVD released for sale on Monday – go to the record shop for nine a.m. as they are going to sell out. Return it back to the shop as there is a crease on the edge of the card covering the DVD case. The replacement has to have a plastic protective covering, get one with this on. Insist, saying it is for a gift for someone – it has to be in pristine condition.

Take the DVD back, he has changed his mind and no longer wants it. Collect magazines from newsagents. Renew rail pass – don't go too early in the day, otherwise they won't renew it for it to start on Monday; go at eight at night. Go back to rail station – he needs fifty timetables of the work journey. He has been banned entering the ticket office due to threatening staff.

Make a list of all the ingredients in ginger biscuits in the supermarket, compare all the different brands, and find out what side effects and damage they can cause the body. He has had one with a coffee, it caused upset in his bowels; he has been poisoned and he needs to know what it is. Go into the bank and get a printed balance statement. Make a list of all the physiotherapists in the area, go to each of the clinics to speak to the physiotherapists directly. Find out if are they smartly dressed. Do they smell? Are they capable of giving him the treatment to the standard that he requires? What are the clinics like inside? Are they clean? Is it in a good area? Phone the doctors and hairdressers for an appointment. It has to be at either of these exact times: 10:14 a.m. or 1:23 p.m. Pick up three cartons of orange juice – this can only be from a family shop 40 miles away. Go to the main library to use one of the computers. Print off all information of his favourite forty actors/actresses about their up and coming projects: films, TV work and any theatre plays they are starring in. On line comic for free – go to library, be there at twelve o'clock to print it off as this is the time it is available to get it for free. Phone his mother to find out what stamps she would like getting to add to her collection.

Go to the toyshop, take photos of toys, and buy toys. Order in store if they haven't got toys he wants there. Write an essay on bowels and related illnesses, and what impact it has on the rest of the body. On and on it goes. Whatever he asks me to do, it has to be fulfilled and he sets the deadline when it has to be completed. Illness, hazardous weather conditions, black ice and snow are all excuses to be lazy which will cause him great upset and further disruption to his life, and I will have to accept the consequences. His list of errands is spiralling out of control, he monopolises all my time. Before he allows me go to bed there is one thing that's been on his mind all through the day. "Why is my wife such a freak? It's not natural to need so much sleep. I think you have a serious mental problem going on here. I don't want to make you cry, you need to pull yourself together with this attitude you have towards me. It is dragging me down, and affecting my confidence. You must really hate me. You didn't close the door correctly last night, don't let it happen again."

The next day, he tests my behaviour through his verbal interrogation which he judges based on the number of hours sleep I had the night before. If he feels I am displaying signs of having an attitude problem towards him, there is the need to reduce my sleep even more. My bad attitude is me showing any form of emotion, being happy or sad without his approval or making my own decision about anything – this could be from turning the washing machine on to making a phone call without asking him first for his permission.

A maximum of five hours sleep keeps me being the kind of person I should be. Damian makes sure most nights I get less sleep by shouting out a list of names of those who have done him wrong. The angrier he gets, the quicker he paces, stamping his feet as he marches back and forth across the landing. Then he starts attacking my bedroom door, shouting out "we know who is going to get it tonight." I lay in bed in fear. My heart is beating ten to the dozen. This is it, he is going to kill me. I have started to barricade myself in my bedroom with the furniture against the door. If he does come in my only escape is to jump out of the window. Then complete silence – no footsteps, no shouting, nothing. Until the buzzing of my alarm clock at five a.m. the start of a new day. The only time when I can be visible to Damian is five forty-five a.m., standing waiting by the door with his overcoat over my right arm. His shoes must be placed to the left-hand side of the bottom step, and a shoehorn placed upright resting inside the heel of the right shoe. My hair must be neatly tied back, discreetly applied make up, and to be smartly dressed at all times in his presence. I am not to be seen or heard whilst he is getting ready for work as he has to focus his mind on the day ahead – an error could cost people thousands of pounds in losses. When he is going to work every morning it is the same routine. 5:55 a.m. I drive him to the train station for him to catch the train to work. I have to be back at the dungeon by six fifteen a.m. to start my cleaning chores – all to be done before I leave to go to work. The entire dungeon has to be cleaned thoroughly – all the paintwork, skirting boards, door frames, windows and windowsills have all to be washed.

All wooden furniture, ornaments and picture frames have to be polished. Floors to be either washed or hoovered, and all of the light fittings to be cleaned and all the bins emptied. The bathroom, kitchen tiles and all units, appliances and fixtures are to be washed, and neatly placed clean towels every day. The slightest bit of dust could be detrimental to Damian's health. The last attack he had, when he was fifteen years old, resulted in him having a rash, and sneezing seizures. Thanks to his mother's rapid first aid treatment, bathing him and applying copious amounts of antiseptic cream prevented him from being hospitalised – she saved his life. So this would never happen again she made sure her husband cleaned the house thoroughly – it was his fault this had happened. Every item or surface had the white glove treatment when she would go on her rounds and inspect for any dust that might harm her son. Like mother, like son, they both suffer the same in so many ways. The parting words given to me every day before he leaves the car to catch the train to work is to be careful, you know what will happen if you don't. He feels it is his duty as a good husband to protect me by telling me that every time I go outside to be on red alert; it is most likely I will be raped at some point in my life. All men will want to rape me because that is what they think when they see someone like me. He has seen photos of horrific injuries as a result of rape, and all the victims have the same thing in common – a certain look and they all look like me. It is pure mental torture for him having this knowledge, and not being there to protect me.

In the event of being raped and possibly murdered, to help the police trace the man or men who killed me, and find my body, Damian feels it is necessary for him to have a written detailed daily itinerary of my whereabouts. This includes the exact times of where I will be throughout the day, how long I will be at a location and the names of any people I am intending to see. This is all to help the police with their investigation, so he tells me. I have to send him text messages throughout the day at the same times written on the itinerary to confirm that I am doing as I have written down. By doing this he can enjoy his day knowing I haven't been raped, and why would I want to ruin his day by not texting him? How cruel would that be to him? The first of the sixty text messages begins when I arrive back at the dungeon at six fifteen a.m. to confirm that I am back inside the dungeon. I check my watch to see it is the correct time to send it. The final text is when I have finished work, and I am inside the car ready to drive home to the dungeon. I have to be back at the exact time on the itinerary – being late, stuck in traffic, is not an excuse, it is an action done with the sole purpose to ruin his day. I made a mistake once by arriving five minutes earlier than I had written down on the itinerary. I was greeted by Damian who pushed me into the wall with his forearm pushing across into my neck, shouting in my face, "Who the fuck are you coming into my house?" If I hadn't have returned early, he wouldn't have done this. It was all my fault, he thought I was a burglar. I should be grateful he hadn't broken my neck. Why did I make him do that?

If I am not careful with my actions I might end up getting him into serious trouble. If I simply stuck to the rules, and adhered to the protocol my life would be so much easier. He tells me he isn't being controlling – it's important to know what the other is doing and to work around each other's routine, it's all about being respectful. Especially for me, I need to learn the etiquette of seeking permission. I am ignorant to such standards due to my upbringing, coming from the gutter. Luckily for me Damian is very happy to teach me the correct standards and explain the rules. The protocol is always to be extremely humble with great gratitude using the correct grammar at all times when addressing Damian, to seek his kind permission to see if he is agreeable for me to do what I am seeking his permission to do. This should be done with gracefulness by showing no emotion or unpleasant tone in my voice. His decision is final. If anything that I am seeking to do will interfere in any of his daily routines it is not allowed.

Rules are the key to life, without them all hell lets loose. By having them, it makes it clear to me what he expects from me, and how I should appropriately act during the routines. Damian introduces his rules and routines daily – they often change. I always need to work harder to try to get it right when doing them. If I tried hard enough, and did as I was supposed to do then there would be no need for Damian to keep continuing telling me where I am failing and going wrong all the time.

I really do try to get it right. The more I try, the more I fail. I am useless. I am not to be trusted, all I say is lies. I need to start acting like a grown-up woman, and not behaving like a child. It's disgusting how I hold my knife, why would I do this to irritate him? It looks like I am going to dissect a body rather than have a meal. I wasn't aware of this until he pointed it out. I make Damian gag so much that he has nearly been physically sick in front of me. It is because I am physically grotesque, and the stench that comes from me is horrendous, especially when I have had a meal. The smell of the food sticks to my hair and clothes, and he can smell it on my breath. This all causes him great pain, and he ends up writhing around on the floor with excruciating stomach pains due to the smell of the food – it causes his body to react this way. The pain lasts for hours – it is so bad he screams out in pain, and eventually passes out because his body can't take any more pain. If the windows are open a burglar will break in and rape me. Air fresheners don't hide the smell. He has talked it over with his mother and the only solution they could come up with is for me to avoid having food that smells. Foods that don't smell are plain yoghurt with blueberries for breakfast, for lunch a lettuce sandwich, one without bread, and for tea a small piece of chicken covered with slices of lemon wrapped in foil cooked in the oven accompanied with frozen peas and carrots and sliced lemon added. All you can smell and taste is lemon. This is my entire diet as well as chocolate. I feel pressurized by him, and his mother to remove foods that smell out of my diet because it causes him to be ill.

To make sure I haven't consumed forbidden foods, he inspects my teeth, and breath upon my return back to the dungeon. I wished there was a pill I could take that would fill me up instead of constantly feeling hungry all the time. Any food I have in the dungeon has to be eaten in the kitchen with the door closed to prevent any food smells escaping, except for chocolate, as he likes to see how much I eat. He would rather I'm anorexic than be fat. I have gone from being a size eight to a size four. Joining the gym is the only thing that I did that pleased Damian. It was my only sanctuary – I went four times a week, the rolls of fat that hangs over my ankles need a lot of work. All I did was run on the treadmill for thirty minutes. Damian thought I did the full circuit programme that was tailored to my fat reduction plan that takes about an hour to complete. The rest of my time there was spent having time to have a shower alone. No Damian sitting there on a stool watching me having a bath, going on about waging another war against someone at work he didn't like. His plan was to go to the park, where the drug addicts hang out and inject themselves with used dirty hypodermic needles that they leave on the floor. He was going to go and pick one up, wondering what type of gloves he would need to wear to protect himself safely to do this. Then he would take it to work, pretend to fall down outside the office at a certain time when he knows this man will be there, as he has been observing this man's routine for the past month.

This man will come over and help him up off the floor. While he is doing this, it is Damian's opportunity to stab him with the hypodermic needle. In his defence he will say he didn't know anything about it, somehow it must have got wrapped in the buckle on his coat cuff, when he was laid on the floor, and then gone in this man's arm who helped him up off the floor. Just think of the mental torture knowing you have three months to wait before they can give you an Aids test to find out if you are infected and all that time just waiting to know you could possibly die. What do I think about it? Inside I feel sick with horror with what an evil bastard he is, planning something like this and this poor man has a wife, and two kids. He doesn't see his own actions as evil or wrong – he can justify to himself that he is right. If he gets found out, so what? It's not his fault, he takes no responsibility for his own actions, it's always someone else's fault. When he went to the Catholic infant school he was a very naughty child, laying traps down so the nuns would slip and fall down. He thought it was fun when they walked over his toy cars that he had placed under the corridor rugs. He liked how they chastised him – a nun would place her hand gently over his, and with a ruler she would hit the back of her own hand that was protecting Damian's hand. She did this until it hurt her, and caused her pain, whilst he stared at her tears running down her cheek. She took his punishment for him whatever he did wrong.

He has always known he is destined to be special, and be greater than anyone for what the caring nun did for him. He can only do the same for me to save my soul. He has to physically hurt himself so as not to physically hurt me, because I cannot do anything right. Remember, the reason why he uses the razor blade to cut into himself is always a result of my actions. Advising him to put the wrong jacket on when it rained and he got soaked, forgetting to buy a pint of milk, shaking when being spat at in the face for making a noise when Damian gave me a burn on my arm and for not looking at him when he was talking. "It's only a game," he says to his mother when she comments about the bruises on my arms wrists and legs. "She likes it." Hmm, that fun game of being held with both my arms pulled straight behind my back, then kicked in my lower back to make me lean forward and swung into a wall. Phew, just missed the wall. Oh, not so lucky, on the fourth and fifth swings I hit the wall. Damian likes the spinning game – he would like to take credit seeing as he invented it. The nuns were right, he is destined to be special. Spin your wife around in circles using her shoulders, keep going for five minutes and ignore her pleas to stop. When she is so disorientated, push her into the walls and then kick her onto the floor, drag her by the legs for at least thirty minutes and cause carpet burns on her back. The best game of all is 'will she or won't she'. When the time is right stand behind using both hands lock them together and place them below the waist. Ensure the tip of the thumb is tucked under the clenched fingers so the knuckle part of the thumb protrudes for greater effect. Then, using a thrusting in and upward direction, forcibly pulling the clenched hands inwards as hard as you can. Remember, your fun may be cut short if your wife can't control her bladder, and urinates not only on herself but you as well. They have to ruin everything you enjoy.

He has gone to a new level of humiliating me whenever we are out together in public. The three-step rule walking behind him has been replaced with him holding my upper arm to drag me along the side of him so he can keep his eye on me. If I don't keep up to his walking pace, he yanks my arm and the pain motivates me to keep up. He uses any opportunity he can to start verbally attacking me if I am not walking quick enough, due to having my foot stamped on which caused a break in the bone on the top of my foot – I heard it snap when it happened. He won't allow me to go to hospital with my foot – it is swollen so much that it is more than double the size it should be and it's so painful that I can hardly walk. I am taking pain relief and bandaging my foot up to my lower leg. When I said I need to have a below knee cast on, and time off work, he snarled, "Who is going to pay your share of the bills?" He certainly wasn't going to. "Would the cast be off in two weeks before the holiday abroad?" I shook my head. Why do I have to ruin everything? There was no way he wasn't going on holiday, I would have to manage. He warned me, "Don't think this will get you out of errands or chores." He gave me more to do. People walking past just stare. It is my fault for showing him up in public. He doesn't care what anyone thinks, he can do what the hell he wants to. Circling around me, shouting, "Do you actually think I like lecturing you every day, telling you what you are doing wrong? Do you think I am that sick?" A man came up to me and asked was I all right? Damian walked up to him and started sizing him up, like two boxers in a boxing ring before the big fight to intimidate each other.

This poor man didn't know what hit him as blood started pouring from the corner of his mouth while Damian stood towering over him with his chest puffed out, looking very proud of what he had done. "Why do people want to speak to you?" What is that about? It's weird. No one ever wants to speak to me. I am the only friend you'll ever have and only ever need. No one else, just me."

My relationship with my mother had come to an abrupt end when she said she only wanted my sister to be her daughter, that I am no longer needed. However she still wanted me to continue paying her bills, cleaning her house, and doing her banking. After fetching her groceries from the supermarket, she insisted that I leave them in the kitchen and she would stay in her bedroom until I had left as she didn't want to see me. She could just about cope seeing me when I drive her in my car to take her for her routine doctor and hospital appointments, but she wouldn't talk to me. She would need help to push her in a wheelchair into the hospital because it's just too far for her to walk. I asked her, does she realise what she is saying to me? She replied, yes. When I refused her demands, she cried, begging me not to stop doing all that I do for her – how will she cope? "Your only daughter will have to do it." She shouted at me, "You know she won't." She confirms what I have always known, deep down but never wanted to accept. She never loved me, and never will. I am nothing to her, I belong with the rest of the scrap and garbage. I am worthless.

For all the tears I have caught rolling from her cheeks, the overdoses, struggles with father, I stood there and fought for her because she was my mum. I loved her. It hurts me inside when I say the words to her, "you will never see me or hear from me again from this moment." Inside, I am shouting out, "come on, Mum, don't do this, it's not right." Only for her to tell me she might as well take another overdose and die, then puts the phone down. My friends have stopped inviting me out to meet up with them as Damian always has something for me to do or he has the weekend away booked. Wherever he goes I have to be there with him, to take photos of him at historic points of interest, pay for everything and fetch him drinks, and to be on hand 24/7 in case he becomes ill. It eases his mother's mind knowing he is not alone, and I can get him medical attention if at any point he needs it. He has been having pains in his bowels and all the tests that four different hospitals can do proved negative. There is nothing wrong. The final conclusion all sixteen consultants could find was that it is in his mind, a mental health problem. His constant aggressive behaviour was marked on his records, as well as the need for security to be nearby. They were reluctant to prescribe medication but, to appease him, they gave into his demands for what he craves – co-codamol and morphine pain relief, on constant long-term repeat prescription as long as he likes. The most important reason why I have to be there is that I am his cash machine – he doesn't carry money. Why bother when he has a rich wife?

He can easily spend three hundred pounds an hour just in a record store on music, films or books. I don't have a proper job – I just sit on my backside listening to bored lonely housewives, according to Damian. He doesn't complain when he is spending all the money I make from my business on clothes, shoes, magazines, collectable toys, golden ticket access at film and theatre conventions at five hundred pounds to meet his favourite actor/actress, and the eighty pounds per signed autographed photograph personally dedicated to him. Not to mention the hotel stay in a five-star accommodation and return rail fare all paid for by me. Damian is very proud and likes to boast how he has never had or needed to have a credit card in his entire life. He doesn't need one because he uses mine, and the pin number to access it is emotional blackmail. If I have run out of cash he doesn't care how much it is, he is having that item. What will cost me more paying for the damage caused by him smashing the entire shop, and its contents or to purchase the item? After all, it is my responsibility to provide for him, and his needs. Then there is two hundred and fifty pounds a month spent on presents for him – these aren't proper gifts, just a token gift; say, a rare limited edition comic.

At Christmas, it takes him two hours to open all of his presents – no less than two thousand pounds is to be spent on him. Holidays are even more obscene with his greed for three thousand pounds to be spent on himself, and gifts for his mother for all that she does for us both, to show her my eternal gratitude for the quiet chats she has with me alone in the conservatory every Sunday, to let me know there are people who are great, and those that aren't so.

"The best way to get on in life and make it so much more easier is by accepting, and knowing your place in society; that you are, and always will be, a slave, there to serve," she advises me while she calmly smiles and pours herself another drink of tea. "Have you seen the cherry blossom on the trees in the garden?"

Did she really call me this or did I hear her wrong? I don't feel I can trust my own sense of judgement any more. Damian sings my praises to his mother – how I am a good timekeeper and never late picking him up from the train station, as well as managing to do his list of errands for him, all to make his life easier. He doesn't know how I do it, what with running my own business full-time. He thanks God every day for how he is blessed to have a wife like me. I think I have a mental problem going on, I really do. Maybe I do need help, maybe it's right what Damian has been saying all along. What is real? Am I dead? Do I exist? I have no idea any more. I pinch myself to confirm that it is real. Half an hour before we arrived at his parents, he insisted there was something he wanted to show me in a field, seeing how it was a nice day to walk there. To get there, you have to cross a busy road. He shouted at me to stay where I was and I did – he ran across the road while I stood in the middle of the road to face an oncoming car. He stood grinning at me on the pavement, watching to see if I would move. He knew I wouldn't without his permission. "Daft bitch, move! You will get knocked down!" I did what I was told to do. He finds this hysterical. After the car has gone, a bus is slowly coming along the road.

Damian stops to point out a song thrush bird in the tree. Can't I see it? The palm of his hand is in the centre of my back and I am instructed to stand at the edge of the pavement to get a better look. Still I can't see it. "What about now?" he yells, pushing me into the road in front of the oncoming bus. The bus swerves to miss me. The bus driver is furious, shouting at me. Damian gestures with his hand, pointing to his own head that

I am not right in the head. I scrambled back onto the pavement and stared at him. I dared to question him. "What have I done to you that is so bad to treat me this way? Why?" "You deserve all the contempt I give you and more. It's like the game of chicken," he laughed; "you get to play it so I can watch. I decide what the outcome is. I can treat you any way I like; you belong to me." All I do is try to adapt to his behaviour to make it through another day. It is only a matter of time – will I be killed by his hand or my own hand? He sucked the life out me till nothing is left, just emptiness. My hopes and dreams he smothered, bound, gagged, and suffocated, all to make me the person he says I should be. A person with no identity, confidence or self-worth, unable to make a simple decision or form an opinion, who is scared of her own shadow. He manipulated and controlled every part of my life so much. If he said go jump off a bridge, I would have done.

Speak no evil, the rise of the seven killings.

A month after my escape from the dungeon, Damian suddenly appeared from out of nowhere. He had been hiding behind the corner of a wall in the car park at the back of the clinic where I worked, waiting for me to come out. I had no idea he was there until I heard his heavy breathing; it's quite distinct how he breathes through his mouth and it made the hairs on the back of my neck stand up. Looking all dishevelled, his clothes all creased, hair not brushed, unshaven, with mud smeared on his cheeks and forehead, he looked like someone going on an army assault training course. Trembling uncontrollably, with his hands clasped together holding them out to me, doing his best 'have pity on me' look, glaring up with his eyes, trying the 'little lost boy look'. All of this just freaks me out even more, I slowly take a few steps backwards to distance myself away from him. He apologised for the way he looks – he had fallen down on a muddy path on his way to see me. He informed me I shouldn't worry as he wasn't hurt, but maybe in a bit of shock. However, it could be due to the cold wind blowing on him, seeing how he has been standing for hours waiting to see me. Not that it mattered, he would have walked barefoot through fire if that's what it takes to get to see his wife again. This is not the Damian I have known for eighteen years. Even more unusual, he is asking if I have got the time to go with him now for a hot drink in a café somewhere nice. Would the real Damian, who held me by the throat shouting in my face "Why should I be nice to you? If you can't try not to irritate me, what do you expect?" please come forward; there is an imposter standing here talking to me.

Alarm bells ring. Why is he being nice to me? What is it that he is after? I don't trust him. I know that his intentions are never sincere. He is planning something, but what? I do know that, in his eyes, he will want revenge, to pay back for what I have done to him for abandoning him – I owe him. How he will do this I am uncertain, whether he will physically, mentally or financially make me suffer. I don't know who is more shocked, him or me, that I said no to his offer. The 'poor me' trembling hands act soon disappeared, as he circled around me, demanding to know why I am telling lies about him. Why would I do this, and make him feel like he is a criminal. My actions have forced him to go to see a solicitor but he couldn't say anything bad about me – he is such a good person, he doesn't have the heart to tell lies about me.

He had received a letter that morning from my solicitor that I had instructed their firm to represent me, and to start divorce proceedings citing Damian's unreasonable behaviour for grounds for divorce. After the solicitor had calculated my monthly outgoings on rent and utility bills, including my half of the mortgage payment for the dungeon, there was no profit, and certainly no money, left for Damian to stake his claim of fifty per cent of my business earnings he threatened to take if I ever left him. It is also in my favour that his outgoings are a lot less, due to only having to pay half of the mortgage, and not having to pay privately to rent somewhere to live as well.

I was advised not to get behind with the mortgage payments on the dungeon, as this is the only item we jointly own together. Basically, it is a straightforward divorce, with a 50/50 split of the sale of the dungeon which they can complete in six months.

Damian is very confident in telling me there isn't a judge in the country that will grant me a divorce, based on the grounds of his religious beliefs – he will never agree to it as it is against his human rights. Damian likes to use the "religion exempt card" to get him out of a troublesome situation. By using, it he can take full advantage of its benefits – never having to work during the Easter or Christmas break because he has to attend the entire church services that can run the entire week. By using Christ, the Son of God, he can secure the guaranteed time off so he could spend it how he wanted which was in the shopping centre.

It's a struggle for Damian living in a quiet suburban three-bedroom fully furnished house, having his laundry done for him and all his meals prepared and cooked by his mother, not to mention having to pay all the utility bills that he simply can't afford. I have a piece of folded cardboard lining the inside of my shoe to stop my foot from getting soaked wet through when it rains. The only furniture I have is a borrowed camp bed, a kettle, a cup, and one fork. The rented flat I live in has no central heating, with damp spreading across the wall and up to the ceiling where it is a marine-green blue colour with spores.

My neighbour on the floor below parties all night, grows and sells marijuana. There is £12.50 in my purse for me to live on for the rest of the week. Half of the dungeon is mine, and so are the bills, even though I am not living there using the water, electric, and gas that is inside a property that I half own, therefore I am obliged to continue paying them according to Damian's calculations. The council tax bill is due – have I got my share of the money to pay for it? Was I aware that missed payments can end up with the owners being sent to prison, and he certainly wasn't going to accept the punishment for it when it clearly wasn't his fault. Damian's distorted story didn't match up when I informed the council tax office that I was no longer living in the dungeon. They updated their records, and would duly contact him as he was entitled to a twenty-five per cent reduction for living alone – even less for him to pay. I wouldn't have to go to prison if he failed to pay because I don't live there.

His surprise visit that he has planned was to try and extort money from me through deception. The lies that flow freely from his mouth is like water running from a tap. Accompanied by such a convincing manner, it's almost like an hypnotic mist in the way he delivers his sugar-coated lies – you actually believe what he is saying. The years he has spent perfecting his technique, all for the greater good that is himself, by believing in his own lies, and distorting the truth is the only way of achieving what he wants – the outcome to be guided by his mentor and tutor, his mother.

She soothes his conscience in justifying it's necessary to go ahead with his sickening plan. He hadn't counted on being interrupted by the receptionist at the clinic where I worked. She had spotted him on her way to work, loitering about at the back of the clinic, and noticed how odd his behaviour was. Assuming that by hanging about at the back of the clinic no one would notice him, ensured he could confront me alone. When he started on his grand finale speech about all that he has done for me, the receptionist came out and asked if this man was bothering me. Should she call the police?

Making decisions is alien to me because he had made all the decisions for me for so many years. Anything beyond my working environment I am at a loss. Trying to recover from the impact of being with Damian isn't easy due to the damage he has caused. I find it extremely difficult to speak, my confidence has gone, and my vocabulary is very limited, I can't think of the words I want to say and when I do speak it doesn't always make sense. Having a relaxed conversation without being in constant fear for saying something wrong is a new experience for me. He did what he has always done, and answered for me. The look of disbelief on his face that the police should be called, declaring he is my husband, and he isn't some sort of rapist weirdo. All I could do was nod my head to confirm what he said was true, the receptionist returned back inside the clinic.

He just carried on with his speech saying the tablets made him aggressive, and do the things he did. He has stopped taking them, and is on a detox programme – he is doing all of this for me. He feels the rage has left him, and is no longer self-harming, he is getting help, he realises it's all got a little bit out of control. Why don't I go with him now to see the doctor so they can explain it all to me? There is no need for a divorce, is there? I am not giving him the answer he wants. The right answer is my answer, my choice – I don't want to be married to him. For me to be a decent person, I must do the right thing, and that is to sign my half share of the dungeon over to him so he is the sole owner, compensation for everything I have put his parents through, the distress I have caused them, and irreversible damage to their health. All of this is taking its toll, especially on his mother – I am the daughter she never had. Just when he had thought he had shaken off the receptionist, she came back outside to check to see if I was all right. They weren't convinced I was all right after watching what was happening outside, they were going to call the police he said he was going, and left.

The next day, I received a letter marked 'Urgent! Read me!' from him. He has come to the conclusion I am having a nervous breakdown. Having thought about it long and hard, he has given me a great life. If he were a woman he would be happy to have a husband like him, one who has never lied to his wife, never sworn in front of her, never punched her and never makes demands sexually.

Clearly I am not of sound mind. Why else would I want a divorce from a man who is the perfect husband? Being the good person he is he has to do something he didn't like doing. Having discussed it with his mother about my mental behaviour, Damian felt he had no option but to come to see me at work to obtain the proof he needed that I was lying about citing his unreasonable behaviour for grounds for divorce. There is no grounds for divorce, it's all in my head. This was his only option – to tape record the entire conversation. It didn't provide him with the evidence he needed to submit to the court, mainly because I hardly spoke. I didn't say the words he wanted me to say, so he couldn't cut and edit the tape.

The entrance road to the car park at the back of the clinic is narrow. You also drive through this road to exit the car park, there is no other way out as it is a dead end. Just before I was due to leave the clinic to go do home visits for the afternoon, I heard a car revving its engine quite loudly, it sounded like someone was having car trouble. I looked out of the window in my treatment room, which overlooks the car park at the back of the clinic. In the car park was a brown car, it had both front passenger car doors wide open, and the front passenger seats pushed forward ready for a person to get into the back seat of the car. Standing at the side of the car was his mother.

Their intentions look clear what they have come to do – even the car was positioned forward-facing for a quick exit. They want me in their car, and will do what is necessary, even to take me by force, so I can be taken back to Damian. This is scaring me, the lengths that he is prepared to go and how far he will go with his actions to get me back, even if it is against my will. There is no way I am going back, I do not want that man or his family in my life.

The receptionist very kindly agreed to go outside with me. I hoped by doing this his parents would go when they saw her. I got in my car and started the car engine. His father drove his car, and angled it in a position to block the exit to prevent me from getting out while his mother ran over to my car, shouting, "What are you doing?" and pulling on the car door handle, trying to open the door that was locked. I pushed down hard on the car horn to make as much noise as I could to draw attention to what they were doing, and in the hope it might even embarrass them, and make them realise what they are doing isn't right. This infuriated his father who got out of the car shouting, "If you don't get out of the car now, then I will make you." I didn't get out of the car. He took a hammer out of his car, and started to walk over to me. It was only when he was instructed to stop by his wife that he did. She noticed the brave receptionist walking over telling them they need to calm down, to talk about things sensibly. His mother agreed saying that is what they have been trying to do, but I have made it difficult for them. They left empty-handed, and his mother a little embarrassed, not by her actions but by her husband's for failing her son.

I waited a little time until they had left, and went to work. I had no option, having been refused legal aid. The pittance that I earn, according to my solicitor, would indeed qualify for legal aid, but they failed to mention to me two very important things about legal aid. Firstly, you cannot get legal aid for a divorce if you are self-employed, and secondly, they class your business turnover as the total amount of money you make in any year as your personal earnings. This is incorrect. In any business, you do not keep all the money you make. You have running costs, rent for room hire, insurance, accountant fees, petrol, supplies, tax, and national insurance – it goes on what you have to pay to keep your business up and running. After all the allowable business expenses have been paid, the remaining money that is left in the pot is your personal earnings/wages, not the entire turnover. For what I personally earn being self-employed, I would be financially better off being employed. I would have the benefit of being paid more, and would qualify for legal aid. If I wasn't working and claiming benefits, I would qualify for legal aid.

I was misinformed, and wasted so much time filling out the appropriate lengthy forms, gathering bank statements, and providing them with further evidence they require about in, and outgoings of my financial life, then refilling the forms again because the advisor doesn't like a decimal point you put on one of the pages. Returning back again with your completed forms with a decimal point they happily accept, but still it can't be sent off because the photocopier isn't working – you will have to come back and re-submit another day. Patiently queuing for forty minutes to see the advisor who demands that there should be today's date on the final bank statement in list of transactions, therefore cannot accept the forms based on this reason. They will not accept a printed statement from the bank due to not having your home address on, and online banking statement is not accepted either. What they are asking is the impossible – we do not have a postal service that can provide your post delivered within two hours of mailing it. Their demands are unreasonable, bureaucracy gone mad; none of it makes any sense, it's a battle you could do without.

A one thousand pound upfront payment on account I have to pay to get my instructing solicitor to start processing the divorce papers, to be served on Damian. At one hundred and seventy-five pounds per hour, not including VAT, all phone calls, emails, appointments made to see my solicitor all incur further costs. Travelling time to attend court hearings, as well as their entire time spent at the court, and transportation of your case notes to the court, and back to the law firm, as well as the court fees, are all further costs that you have to pay. The estimated cost for the divorce, and the financial settlement, is six thousand and five hundred pounds. I need all the money I can earn with no family support to help me financially.

No savings – Damian made sure of that when he spent everything I earned, and more, which has got me into three thousand pounds of debt. This is not his problem, the credit card is in my name. Then there is the constant tiredness. I am feeling just so exhausted all the time, finding it difficult to carry on working. Some days, by the time it's ten a.m., I feel so drained that I don't have the energy to carry on but I have to as I can't afford to take any time off – no work, no money.

Another 'Urgent! Read me!' letter. He doesn't trust the postal system. Not only does Damian send letters to my work place he also makes the journey to walk into my solicitors, and hand delivers a duplicate copy of them to the receptionist for them to pass them on to me. He has come to another conclusion as to why I have left him – not having children has made me a cold, heartless and uncaring woman. He thinks he would make a great father. I need to bear his children so he is prepared to have sex with me. My solicitor seems to think he is just having difficulty in letting go because he loves me so much. It's not love, he is after revenge – he likes it sweet and served piping hot on a plate, preferably with my beating heart. The divorce procedure isn't moving quick enough – four weeks of valuable time wasted through applying for legal aid, which was never an option for me, when the papers could have already been served on him. Finally the papers are ready to be served by a court bailiff, or process server – it is a private courier service for legal papers. I have to contact them to organise when they are to go to the dungeon to personally serve the papers. Damian will be handed the papers physically and, by accepting the papers, it is acknowledgment of being served them.

Once he has been served, it takes six weeks and one day for the decree nisi – they give you this amount of time in case you change your mind. Then after this time you can apply to the court for your decree absolute, which is a certificate saying you are now divorced.

I explained to the process server that it may be difficult to serve on Damian. What with the six-foot iron gates being constantly locked, they will have to climb over them to get access to the front door. With his aggressive behaviour, and self-harming, the chances of him opening the front door are zero. He knows how the legal system works, and how to play it at it's own game. He certainly does not agree to the divorce, and will never accept the divorce papers being served on him. Refusing to have the papers or running away from the process server, is deemed as being served on as the process server verbally conveys what they are doing. The process server needed time to talk to the police regarding their own safety, to help them decide whether they would go ahead and serve the papers on Damian due to his self-harm with Stanley knife blades. What would be the likelihood of Damian attempting to slit their throat, or stab them? The process server demanded to know how at risk they were, I can't say no he wouldn't – if he felt pushed into a corner, he might take drastic steps. How, I don't know; what is in his head is not normal. It was agreed that in an attempt of an attack, the police could be at the dungeon within minutes to help the process server, and taser Damian who would be taken into custody.

Several attempts were made throughout the day to serve on Damian and each time they went to the front door and knocked, Damian did not open the door. The next option to try and serve on Damian was for the process server to do a stake-out in their car, a bit like what the TV shows portray American cops do, with the box of donuts, and huge cup of coffee waiting for the culprit to come out of the building so they can arrest them. Five hours into the stake-out, there was still no sign, but the court requires all the evidence to prove that every possible action has been taken to serve the papers, even though I know it is going to be a waste of time and more money. I don't agree with it but it is how it is. I have to accept it, and trust in the legal system.

Another important message, except this one came from his mother. It needed to be passed directly on to me as soon as I arrived at the clinic. Damian has been rushed into intensive care, having suffered a stroke. They were holding a bedside vigil, and I should be there with him. It is odd that she had called my mobile only minutes earlier to leave another abusive message, no mention about Damian just her usual favourite two words "die bitch." At least I know where he is, I just had to get the ward, and room number from the hospital admissions to find Damian so the process server could pay him a visit on my behalf.

I phoned six hospitals, only to be informed by each of them that there was no one there of that name. They even checked under his date of birth, and the dungeon address to see if he had been admitted. He wasn't in any of them, so where was he? All was revealed the next day by an 'Urgent! Read me!' letter. He had left the area, and he was no longer living at the dungeon because he cannot afford the house, utility bills or the upkeep. He was now living in convents, but will not say where he is, as he feels he is under constant threat of divorce. He is no longer working as the law firm got rid of him because he broke the terms and conditions in his contract by getting ill.

He hasn't got long left to live, just a matter of months. The nuns say they can cure him, and he believes they will, but, for this to happen, I have to stop the divorce proceedings – it's my decision whether he survives or dies. He realises the huge pressure I must be feeling right now and he wouldn't want me to struggle. In order to help me, he has drawn up a contract that puts his mother in complete control of the dungeon. Any issues concerning the dungeon all have to go through his mother's approval, even if I want to tend to the garden outside, or go inside, I have to be granted permission from her first. Otherwise I will be treated like a trespasser, and the police will be called to have me physically removed from the property. There will be someone there 24/7, mainly his parents staying separately alternate nights to guard the dungeon from burglars. His mother is a registered disabled person who is housebound due to the crippling effects of raging arthritis riddled throughout her entire body, causing so much pain that she is incapacitated.

She can barely walk more than three steps unaided and requires constant daily care from the minute that she wakes up. She has to have her medication brought to her because she gets so confused over which tablet to take and might accidentally take an overdose. Due to one of many adverse side effects, the main ones being extreme drowsiness and dizziness, which can cause a problem with a sense of judgement and making important decisions. Not safe to be left alone, all meals need to be prepared and cooked for her. Help is especially needed for all aspects of all personal hygiene due to her debilitating condition. How can someone be expected to stay alone in a three-bedroomed house, have to climb up a flight of stairs to go to bed, use the bathroom, and be on guard to fight like a ninja to ward off any burglars? Impossible, if a person were that genuinely ill. To help cover up his own lies, he is in turn exposing his mother's, who has been claiming for the past twenty-five years disability allowance. Without it, there would be no holidays three times a year to race up the famous Whitby Abbey's one hundred and ninety-nine steps. I am so angry at him – he takes no responsibility for anything. Is he going to pay the mortgage, or am I going to have to pay it all while he sings songs with a nun who plays the guitar? A returned letter was sent back to my solicitor, with big letters scrawled on it from his mother, commander and chief – she isn't to be contacted about trivial things to do with the dungeon, is this understood? That's the reply to my question I had to instruct my solicitor to write, and ask if her son was going to pay his share of the mortgage.

To progress further with the divorce will be difficult without his residing address. The solicitors have a duty of care to inform a person that legal action is being taken against them so that they can obtain to seek legal representation and make sure that the case is fair, not one sided. In order to do this, there has to be some way of contacting that person, so they are fully aware. A contact address is the key to success.

The endless errands Damian had me running in all directions for him have now been replaced by trawling through the lengthy letters he sends, trying to find clues to his location. Any clues I do find, I chase them up – phoning monasteries he mentions, or contacting the hotels he may have possibly stayed at from letters he has written on the hotel letter headed paper, and more hospitals to which he has been admitted due to having had another stroke which has resulted in him being bedridden, unable to walk or talk. It didn't stop him travelling to London – how ever did the station porter manage to wheel him on to the train, in the hospital bed, I will never know. All of this is encroaching upon my time at work and, if that isn't enough, during the evening I have to read through the bundle of papers my solicitor has prepared to be submitted to go to court. Before it can be submitted, it has to be sworn in, they call it an affidavit. It's evidence of everything that has been tried to locate Damian, from the process servers and their written evidence about the several attempts at numerous times throughout the day, to the private investigator's findings. They couldn't locate him – no response from the newspaper advert or from the letter sent to his workplace. His friend confirmed he hadn't seen or spoken to him since Christmas. His parents sent a rather aggressive letter stating they are being harassed by my solicitor and, if this continues, they will take legal action. They do not know where he is, and haven't had any contact from him. I do not believe them, they know where he is, and they are hiding him because he is living with them.

Due to the government cuts to save money, the family law building that only dealt with matrimonial, family issues, and the commissioner of oath office that was situated here for you to swear your affidavit has closed. So all hearings are now held in the county court, as well as hearings ranging from motoring offences, burglary, shop lifting, grievous bodily harm to drug offences, and many more – the list goes on. The commissioner of oath office also was relocated to the county court building. To help reduce the costs of my rapidly increasing legal fees, rather than my solicitor going, I went instead. I didn't have to make an appointment, I just turned up. I took some extra time off work as my solicitor said it was extra busy since the relocation. I felt very uncomfortable as I walked up the steps to the county court. Standing outside either side of the entrance door, was a group of about seven men with gaunt faces. All in uniformed tracksuit attire with the obligatory baseball cap, and smoking a cigarette that didn't smell like it contained tobacco.

They were standing there on their smoke break, while waiting to be called in for their hearing. One of them looked me up and down as I passed by, commenting how he liked his pussy to be with thick cream. Grinning at me, he said, "She is a new court bitch, not seen her here before." He puckered his lips together. "Come here, puss, puss, let me stroke you." I know I have to go into the building but I don't find it easy. I should not be intimidated or be talked at in a derogatory way.

I was expecting to be ushered into a room to take the stand, and hold the Bible given to me by the gowned court usher; to say, "Swear by Almighty God this is the whole truth, nothing but the truth, so help me God, amen" in front of the judge. The small room I entered had two cashier screens, like you get in a bank where you place your cash in the well so the cashier can get it and slide a tray across to your side of the counter so they can access your money. This is how they pass you the Bible and the card with the oath to read from – that's it. My sworn written statement that sets out the evidence that we wish to give to the court, and what we are seeking from the court is a request that we dispense the service of petition. In other words, it is impracticable to serve as they can see from the evidence submitted. A district judge has the authority to grant the divorce papers as being served, if they feel enough has been done in their opinion. The court order states that both parties are required to attend the hearing on the set date and time specified, with their legal representation to be there an hour before the hearing.

Just reading this brings me to tears. Not only will he be there sitting staring at me, but also trying to intimidate me. My biggest worry is not being able to speak, and get my words out. Some days aren't that great – on a bad day, I can't speak; maybe a noise or nothing at all, only more tears pouring out that I can no longer hold back or control. This is what worries me. It has taken nine months of gathering evidence to submit to the court – I don't want to ruin this opportunity. I have to speak up, no one is going to do this for me. It's a chance to be heard – whether they will believe me is another one of my worries.

I sat waiting for my solicitor inside the county court waiting room, on the toughened plastic bench bolted into the ground. It looked more like an industrial warehouse with the bare exposed concrete walls, not what I imagined the inside of a county court to look like. Neither was I expecting it to be so busy – with the noise of the conversations being openly exchanged between solicitors with their clients, discussing how to get them off the charges that have been made against them. A woman had violently kicked her dog so much while high on drugs that she killed it. She was sitting to my left side on the bench, and on my right side of the bench, high on heroin and ecstasy, a man up for GBH offences with his solicitor trying to convince him to come clean to the judge; if not, he will be looking at five years prison sentence. To think how

Damian berates people like this, and refers to them as the dregs of society that bleed our economy dry.

If he had his way he would put them all, including everyone below his standards, and particularly anyone that is disfigured, into gas chambers like Hitler did to the Jews. Damian's hunger for morphine and violence makes him the same, except he hasn't been tried for his crimes.

All family, and matrimonial cases hearings are held in front of either residing district judge one, district judge two or district judge three. Who will be sitting in to hear your case is not always the one stated on the court order. Damian failed to turn up at the hearing, he didn't even send a solicitor to represent him on his behalf. Instead, just a few hours before the hearing, he made sure I received a written letter from a Sister at a Birmingham convent, who was only too happy to write on behalf of Damian. She hoped I would receive her letter, before it was too late, in order to prevent the terrible decision I am making in trying to end what is a sacred union between a man and wife. She and Damian have spoken at great lengths about me. All the nuns in the convent are praying that we be reconciled together, and be reunited as man and wife, for she understands how it can be easy to lose our path in life. 'Trust in the Lord, He will guide you; accept His love, and your sins will be forgiven', she implores. Damian knows full well about court hearings, although matrimonial law is not what he is practiced in. He can, however, access information through legal organizations that can give information. He has access to everything he needs to know, including case histories of past divorce cases that were successful and those that weren't.

Had I not submitted this letter in the hearing, and brought it to the attention of the district judge, it would have been seen as an unfair disadvantage against Damian, because this new evidence might lead to his whereabouts, allowing him to be personally served upon. The law states in this country everyone has the right to a fair hearing with access to legal representation. You must be duly notified about it, either personally served or through the post to your home address or current address. District judge one examined all the submitted evidence, including two of Damian's letters that he had handwritten to me, stating that he doesn't agree to the divorce, never will, and that he was no longer living in the area or working any more. He admitted how controlling he had been towards me – this incriminating evidence was all there in black and white. The detailed log book was provided by the process server, documenting times throughout the day that they attended the dungeon to attempt to serve the divorce papers, and to no avail. District judge one would not grant an application to dispense for service, and suggested that we make an application to court, for alternative service due to the letter from the Sister at the convent. Alternative service is to serve him in any place where he is happening to be staying, not a fixed home address. District judge one recommended by doing this, it enables the bailiff to serve him the papers directly to him at the convent. My solicitor pointed out the difficulty we have had tracing him, as it's not conclusive that he is still there in the convent.

To which district judge one came to the conclusion "He is struggling, and clearly loves you. It's probably not what you want to hear." No, I didn't come to hear their opinion on what they deem love is. What is quite concerning is that district judge one, after reading his letters, thinks abuse is a clear indication of his undying love for me. Even more worrying is that district judge one has the power and the authority to assess who should be granted a divorce. I personally don't feel they are mentally capable of assessing the situation. The district judge's hands are tied, that's all my solicitor will comment on the outcome of the hearing.

Getting the papers served at the Birmingham convent was no longer an option, seeing how Damian was no longer there. He had to return back home for medical treatment for the pain he was having with the terminal cancer. What with the very little time he had left on this earth, he felt it important to go to the convent to confess his sins. Was God going to send him to purgatory or to ease his conscience for all he has accomplished in life, every action was a necessary one. The Sister at the convent was deeply touched by Damian's sentiments, given the condition he is in – making the journey alone is difficult to reach them at the convent, with the little strength he has and facing his imminent death without his family. Such strength in a person is a rare and precious gift – to carry on for your loved ones, and not let them see your suffering is a heavy burden.

As difficult that we may find it, for some it's not natural, we all need to find it in our hearts, and help those less fortunate and especially those who are suffering. Having spent time together praying morning, noon and night the Sister had come to know Damian quite well during his time that he stayed at the convent, for the Lord works in mysterious ways, and guided him there to her, to the discreet hidden convent miles from anywhere, encased by a twenty-foot stonewall that is covered with ivy, and surrounded by trees and overgrown shrubs. It is situated down a winding road that you wouldn't know is there. Poor satellite reception that means your satellite navigation in your car and mobile phone are useless. No visitors are allowed in the convent unless you have prior consent from the Sister. Out of all the convents there are in the country, God chose this one for Damian – he had nothing to do with it.

I contacted all the hospitals again, and the local hospice to see if he had been admitted – nothing. So where is he now? His letters are just long rants, informing me from now on he will be only sending one of God's representatives to contact me – a nun. He only answers to God, only God can judge him, God's law is final, there is not a court of law in this country that can judge him or make him do what is forbidden in the eyes of God. There are no clues to his current whereabouts. Based on the new evidence that he is no longer at the convent, and details to prove this was submitted to district judge one at the second hearing, who ordered that we apply to the court for a further application for alternative service through his employers, even though he is no longer working there, due to having a stroke which district judge one was fully aware of, having sat on the bench at the previous hearing. To prove this course of action isn't going to get the papers served, I asked my solicitor (they are the only ones who can speak to the district judge; you are not allowed unless they address you, then you can speak) to ask district judge one to let me phone his employers on speaker phone in front of them now, to confirm does he, or does he not, work there. I was refused on the grounds it needs to be in writing, and submitted to the court at the next hearing. A district judge's decision is final – if I want to appeal it, to be aware that it might not help my case, and go against me, and then there is the increase in my legal fees. I am damned if I do, and damned if I don't, blackmailed by the legal system that is supposed to be there to help, it makes a mockery of the whole system. What happened to everyone being entitled to a fair unbiased trial, the scales of justice, and equal rights? This clearly only applies to Damian, who blatantly lies to the court, and confirms this in his letters. He even walks into my solicitor's office and hand delivers to the receptionist more letters for me to read, not once but on four separate occasions, days before the next court hearing while still pretending to be living at another convent.

This just happens to be in Ireland, where he has successfully completed a course and is now fully qualified as a religious education teacher. He is ready to go into schools, and teach children the Catholic morals. It is highly unlikely he will be able to return back to live in the dungeon for the foreseeable future, due to being unable to walk or talk due to the stroke he suffered. What does the legal system do, they allow him to continue in what he is doing. This just feeds his ego showmanship. Look at me, what I am doing, I can do what the hell I want to and you can't do a thing, he parades his web of deceit in the face of the district judges. Actually, they can do something about this, so why do they choose not to?

At the third hearing, district judge two contemplates their thoughts out loud, regarding the contents of the delivered letter from Damian that morning. Has he done this with clear intent? Has he the mental capacity to understand what he is implying? Is he qualified enough to make this statement by being

101

educated, or has he simply got learning disabilities? Is that the issue here?

Written in block capitals: *YOU HAVE NOT SUFFERED ENOUGH WITH THE DIVORCE. I INTEND TO MAKE YOU PAY FOR WHAT YOU HAVE DONE, AND I WILL MAKE YOU SUFFER MORE..* It's a clear message. He is a very educated man with six law degrees, and is a fellow of the legal executives, and a commissioner of oath. There is no doubt to his ability, or to his mind. How much more evidence do you need?

District judge two requires further evidence that this wasn't a spur of the moment, one-off random letter, that he could have easily sent by mistake, as he wasn't there to answer the question. To prove this wasn't a random letter, it is in fact one of many and there is no mistake in what he is doing, I had to submit another letter for the district judge two to read, before they made their final decision at the hearing.

In view of his written comments, he knows how I want to be in control, and he will never let that happen. He is never going to let the divorce happen. I am more like a mother, and a big sister to him. If we could not be together in life, then he will make sure we would soon be reunited together in death. District judge two finally granted a decree nisi, concluding he is fully aware of what he is doing. Just six weeks and one day to decree absolute, then I will be finally divorced from Damian. I can't believe it's finally happening.

One week and one day to the divorce being finalised, an appeal was lodged at the county court from a National Health Service nurse, who bears a striking resemblance to Damian's mother. In between looking after patients, working long shifts due to the government cuts, and being under staffed on the wards, a nurse has taken the time during her busy shifts, to find out the court hearing reference number relating to the hearing when the decree nisi was granted.

This number was quoted in the top corner of the letter on a non-letterhead piece of paper, followed by the words 'this patient should not have a divorce, he is too ill. Do not contact his parents, he no longer has a mobile phone, and he cannot be gotten hold of. I have never received any documents about the divorce, this is the first I have heard of it, and the court is taking advantage of an ill man, yours, anonymous.' Even more remarkable – his mother and the nurse share the same writing and dialogue. It's almost like they are one and the same person.

The court decided to allow Damian a proposed appeal, which means the decree nisi is rescinded (in other words, cancelled), based on this letter. How can he physically, and mentally go ahead with a proposed appeal? It's impossible for him to, because if he is so ill, too ill that he can't write or speak, and a nurse has lodged an appeal for him as, which is clearly stated in the appeal, his parents won't be getting involved. The court requested, for the appeal, an up-to-date medical report, and confirmation of his address. Where will the court send this request to? The unknown nurse who made the appeal from the unknown hospital? No, they are sending it to the dungeon and, in anticipation, wait for him to respond. It's all on his terms and his rules; he decides when to get in contact. Can the court not see what he is doing is unreasonable given all the evidence submitted for the past eighteen months?

How he has been continually evading giving his fixed address or his whereabouts, not only to the court but also to the police? They have been trying numerous times to contact him about the excessive letters he continually sends to me, full of verbal abuse, continual emotional blackmail, and implied threats of violence, all intended to mentally torment and harass me. You would think if you are dying would you have the energy or the desire to do all of this? Is this how you would choose to spend your time living the final days of your life? Damian's imminent death, and having terminal cancer is a surprise – he has only months, maybe days, to live. He has sent me cards to read, only to be opened on his passing. His filed medical report submitted to the court has a very different opinion of Damian's health. There is no mention of Damian having a diagnosis of being terminally ill with cancer and it has been such a long time since his registered GP has seen him. The court concluded that they believed he did reside at the dungeon, due to the police attending the dungeon to deliver an harassment order, a letter telling him not to contact me which they left in the post box. This confirmed their belief and the decree nisi was re-instated. This was appealed again by Damian in a ten-paged dossier sent to the court for their immediate and urgent attention.

He had no knowledge of the divorce proceedings, having never received a divorce petition. Neither has he received an acknowledgement of service or any decree nisi.

This is the first time he has heard of the decree nisi being re-instated. Why is this then he has not been notified, and been excluded from giving his point of view? Is it simply because of his state of health? He stated that I was kept fully up-to-date with his whereabouts, the hospitals, and the sisters at the convents had phoned me at regular intervals to keep me up-to-date with his condition. Due to the state of his current health, he is too ill to walk or talk, and couldn't possibly attend court, as he would need considerable assistance in doing so. Despite my unforgiving cruel nature, he believes in the sanctity of marriage, and it has been suggested to him that we attend marriage counselling through the Catholic Church. How could he have possibly attended a court hearing when he was an in-patient in hospital? Are the courts aware of this? He has been advised that all post sent to the dungeon was all returned back to sender, including post from the courts, and my solicitor which they should have been aware of, so how can he respond to something he has never had? He claims the court is lying that they have served him and he wants proof of this, including all the times and dates. He wants the court to be aware that he may not receive their letters due to the dungeon not being his fixed address. He can't state at what time of day when he will be in hospital or in a convent, so, if the court requires his location in England or Wales to serve him, he would need to know in advance.

Why isn't he being treated the same as me? It's unfair that my address is kept confidential, when I know his address because he has provided it to me.

It's appalling the way the courts are treating him, they have failed to correctly serve him – he has had no involvement whatsoever. He's accusing the courts of having lied by saying it's not been done correctly when it has. He also accuses myself, and my solicitor, that we have withheld evidence from the court, stating that we were fully aware of his hospital admissions, and of the times he has stayed in the convents. Must he have to remind the court that is illegal, especially with

105

knowing that he would never receive any information? This was done solely with the pure intention of someone trying to get their own way, this should not be tolerated. As a vulnerable patient this does not give the law the right to treat him this way.

He is now classed as being disabled, which has been certified due to the abuse that people shout at him when he is out in the streets, he can only describe it as disability name calling. As a result of having not one, but two strokes, he is now unable to hold or use a telephone, which he no longer has use for. I didn't leave him because he was unreasonable, it was because of his ill health, which was due to the prescription medication that he was taking and the side effects that caused him to have paranoia and pressure over his skull. Only the doctors, and the hospitals are capable of assessing his state of his health, and to whether he has the capacity (whatever this may mean, he doesn't fully understand the meaning of the word) to attend any court hearings – It is not the decision of the court.

Damian is somewhat confused at the court's remarks referring to the police's involvement in this divorce case. He has never been offensive in anyway, or committed a crime, nor has he ever been arrested. In his entire life he hasn't been questioned by the police. The only time he has spoken to them was during his time when he was a practising lawyer. In what respect are the court saying the police have attended the dungeon to serve the petition, because if this is the case they have never done so. Whatever has been implied has not happened, or taken place. He finds it difficult to believe the police would lie about such a thing. If someone has lied about him, or if the police are stating untruths about him, he requires their full details in order to lodge a complaint about them.

The only cards he has sent to me are on my birthday, and at Easter. He fails to see how this could offend anyone – it was bought from a Christian shop. He always sends them to my solicitor or my place of work, never to my home address, to give me space. During his time in the legal profession for many years, he is aware of the procedures and seems to have doubts over my solicitor, and the process server's ability. He requires a detailed full chronological order of all of the so-called evidence, including every statement containing anything that is negative towards him personally. He wants his chance to at least defend himself against those who have lied, and by doing so trying to damage his good reputation and character.

To prove to the court my mental state is questionable, he submitted a letter that I had written to him shortly before I left. He doesn't like sharing with strangers these personal letters from me, but, in order to show the court my on and off opinion towards him, he feels he has no option. He also feels threatened, and intimidated by my behaviour, due to the disturbing messages I often send him, which he feels is due to my state of mind. In light of this evidence, he trusts that the matter will be resolved. There is a moral responsibility and he trusts the court will take this into account.

Three days after the court received this lengthy dossier, Damian is like a dog with a bone, he is not letting it go, he needs to know they understand him by putting pressure on them. He sent four more lengthy ten-paged dossiers full of the same comments, demanding to know why are the courts not doing as he asks of them. As a result, the courts have asked him to stop sending any correspondence to them, they will no longer accept any post sent from him. They hoped by doing this it would then force him to seek legal representation, who would confirm to the court the details of his address for service. Damian is fully aware of what they are trying to do, and reminds the court that, in order to get the correct legal representation, he needs to know first what is being implied against him. He would require to be sent to him, all documented evidence against him to help him decide what legal action is required.

Never before has the county court experienced any case like this. You would think there were millions of pounds that he was trying to protect. It's not a spectacular case, just a divorce and a basic house – that's it. Damian definitely got the court's attention – he says jump and they respond to his demands. They have allowed him a proposed appeal, to be heard in front of one of the district judges, so he can defend himself against these allegations. The law is so vague, it's not clear, and it's very much open to interpretation, that's why you get very different opinions from different district judges.

Both dispensed, and alternative service have been deemed served. Normally, it is either one or the other, never both, and decree nisi granted not once but twice, then cancelled. Three things the court fear – Damian is a former solicitor, and he has the top cards in his pack already. He has made it clear he is defending himself in the divorce and not even the court can make him get legal representation. By using these cards he can do whatever he wants, and he clearly pointed out to them in a law article that there is an undefined amount of times he can appeal – there's no limit to it, which he intends to use to his full advantage. As well as using the disability card plus the litigation card, it's a full house; it's a win-win combination.

District judge three wafts in mid-air a letter submitted to the court, an hour before Damian's proposed appeal, explaining his absence from the hearing due to a blood transfusion, is demanding to know if this letter genuine, seeing how it's not on official hospital letter headed paper. It is simply not good enough, and he suspects that it is not an original. Why would he send a genuine one in, it would be so out of character. The court have been more than happy in accepting fake ones, and have never questioned it or the other evidence submitted. They didn't even work out the calculations to figure that the sequence of events don't tally up. District judge three ordered that Damian write to the court with all details of address for service. The court requires a further medical report from his treating doctor, with full details of his current health, their opinion of his ability, both physical and mental, to whether he can attend court. All of this has to be submitted again to the court, and they will then consider his appeal. If he fails to do this within two weeks, my solicitor will be able to apply for the decree absolute.

My heart sank when my solicitor informed me that Damian's medical report had been submitted at the court. They were still waiting for his address for service to be submitted. The court had already decided they would grant him his appeal based upon his medical report, despite his treating doctor (the one you prefer to see, not the one who they register you with, when you first join the medical practice as a patient) had not seen him for a long while. It was over a year ago when Damian had last visited the doctor's surgery, displaying odd symptoms with heavy arms, and weak legs, and he spoke with a speech impediment.

An MRI scan on his brain proved normal, so the consultant wondered if it was just stress related. Other than painful bowels, no other medical condition was found. However, his father and the doctor agreed that Damian was too ill to mentally and physically attend court hearings. Due to the harassment the county court are experiencing from Damian, the hearing has already been transferred to another court. This has now become an out of control situation, the court were at a loss as what to do. By doing this, it finally puts an end to it. For who, the court or me? For this type of hearing my solicitor has to instruct a member of council, a barrister (they argue for you and make it difficult for the person they are questioning, so they tell the truth – they actually win awards for this) for the proposed appeal. To represent my case in front of the judge, Damian will have to be questioned under oath by the barrister, so that he will speak only the truth. If he is found in contempt of court with his version of events, based on the evidence my solicitor has previously submitted to the previous county court, they may lock him up.

Wednesday morning – the day of the hearing. I wasn't required to be at the hearing, so I went to work as usual. My solicitor would contact me after the hearing to let me know the judge's final decision. Not the phone call I was expecting to receive – a phone call from a CID police officer. They were outside my home, trying to contact me to inform me that a person walking their dog had found Damian unconscious, with stab wounds, in a field not far from the dungeon. It happened quite early that morning.

He was admitted into intensive care in a critical condition and, at the moment, they suspect that it could be attempted murder. Could I give them some background to Damian's personality? I could only tell them how he was with me, that he might be different with his friend, that he self-harms with a Stanley knife on a regular basis, but I had not spoken to him for over two years as we were no longer together and were going through a lengthy divorce. The officer asked would I go into the police station to give them a character statement about Damian. I contacted my solicitor to inform them what had happened, who directly informed the court about the incident, that due to the circumstances Damian was unable to attend the scheduled hearing that morning. A detailed statement had already been submitted to the court, personally delivered by Damian's mother. You would have thought she had a law degree or three based on how it was prepared. It stated that it must be brought to the court's immediate attention that I have been taken into police custody for questioning for the attempted murder of her son, for this to be on record at the court and my actions in all of this. My actions for what? What have I done that is so bad that this is justified punishment for me, to be falsely accused of a crime I didn't commit? I am deeply offended by this and her actions. By signing it, his mother accepts full responsibility and confirms her entire involvement in abetting fraud, in itself is a criminal offence during any legal proceedings, and perverting the course of justice.

I fail to see if you have not been informed that your son was in a specific hospital, how would you know he was there, unless you have prior knowledge to the sequence of events that were about to take place. The knife used to stab Damian hadn't been found and the police were trying to trace it, as it may lead them to the attacker. All avenues had to be tried, even going through the dungeon inside and out, as well as door to door enquiries, but it didn't lead them any nearer to finding the attacker. A resident across from the fields, did however confirm that Damian would regularly go down to the fields to feed the horses every morning, like clockwork, at six a.m. and that he had done so for the past two years. This further confirms where he has been all along, hiding in the dungeon.

After I had given a character statement about Damian, the CID officers felt my safety was an issue. I confirmed the locations on his body where he had previously cut himself, which tied in with the comments of the doctors at the hospital. They had noticed scarring on the areas I had mentioned. The doctors at the hospital felt the location and angle of the superficial stab wounds indicated that they were self-inflicted by Damian, so did the police, proving it is a different matter. They have a duty of care and obviously have to investigate. If he did really get attacked, and the attacker struck elsewhere then the police would be in serious trouble and be sued. Damian's version of events were vague about what happened, but it gave the police an insight into Damian's world – abandoned, victimised, and the world owes him a living.

Because of how he treated me during our relationship, and given his mental state (it's not normal to cut yourself with a Stanley knife blade), they felt the attack was aimed at me, a shock tactic to control me further, and I could be at risk from being attacked. They wanted me to be aware that he is being discharged in the morning, twenty-four hours after being admitted into intensive care, as the doctors are happy with his recovery. My head is spinning. How can that be, if what they are saying is true and they believe the injuries are self-inflicted? Surely they need to keep him in for psychological assessment? Other than displaying an intensely close relationship with his mother, which the nurses have commented on, his parents have denied that he self-harms, so there is nothing they can do, they can't detain him under the Mental Health Act. There is no definite evidence that the police can find either way, regardless of what they suspect – the court requires firm evidence to show the judge, otherwise it will get thrown out of court. If Damian decides to take his actions further against me physically, then they would have a case; otherwise, their hands are tied. Nothing is connected to him. I never reported it to a doctor or the police about being strangled or how he threatens to remove my fingernails with a fork, or how he instructs me to hit myself while he sits, and watches. It might sound stupid, but I honestly didn't know that how he was treating me was abusive. It becomes a way of life, you become so accustomed to it that you accept it as a normal part of everyday life.

On the day Damian was discharged from the hospital, police protection unit (PPU) were very quick to get in touch with me to inform me of his discharge, CID had informed them of the serious incident involving Damian. Was I aware how serious it was? Because of what Damian had done, they felt my safety was at risk. As a result they have been assigned to be my PPU officer. They needed to get a background picture firstly of my relationship with Damian, just a few questions, it would only take thirty minutes.

It was a little difficult as I was about to see a client in a few minutes, but I had more time the next day to answer any questions as I had a gap in between two appointments. There and then, they had to advise me to ring 999 if I saw Damian, and to be aware there is a high probability that he will try and kill me. Have I heard right? Maybe I misunderstood what this police officer was saying. I hadn't at all. How do you digest those words when someone tells you your life is at danger and they can't do a thing about it until the attack happens? Based on my answers during the detailed series of questions, they were able to assess what category risk factor I fell into. They could even predict my cause of death – that he would kill me through strangulation. Due to this, it puts me at an even greater risk, therefore they had placed me on the High Risk register with the PPU. My home address, and work address had a tag placed on it – this means priority response linked to being at High Risk, in case the police were called to go to either of these locations.

They need to provide me straight away with a GPS sky guard unit. It is a mobile tracking device, so they can physically find me, and I have to wear it under my clothes at all times when I go outside. In the event of being attacked or possibly murdered, firstly press the button on it, to start it recording. Run as fast as you can and, while running, dial 999. Tell them your location – the more details they have, the sooner they can find you, but keep running. By now the recording will have gone through to one of the police centres,

114

where they will hear, and log the details of events leading up to, and including my death. If they haven't managed to get to me in time, and I am killed, they will be able to trace my body, providing the tracking device is still on my corpse. The recording will be used as evidence against Damian to get him convicted in a court of law. My mind can't process these words. These words, spoken as a matter of fact, almost a sure thing, a definite certainty that this is going to happen. So I am to be reassured that wearing a tracking device makes this OK, and that being prepared for what is about to happen will take the fear away or it will make the pain any less than what it will be? Is this supposed to help me knowing that in the event of my murder, the two hands responsible for taking my life will be a hand of a man they knowingly allowed to murder me, and the hand of the antiquated laws that form our entire legal system will have killed me, and countless others, in what could have been prevented. That's it! Nothing can be done, there are no laws preventing this, I have to accept what is to be.

All the PPU can do is provide me with leaflets and advise me on safety issues. Nothing is guaranteed in protecting you. It's all down to you, in implementing the necessary actions in safeguarding yourself from being attacked, not only now but also in the future. The key to success is remaining on constant guard and living an invisible life, almost like you have fallen off the edge of the earth. To eliminate any traces of yourself from all records that can possibly link you to your potential murderer – it's the only way to prevent them from tracking you down and killing you. This means changing your entire name, where you live, possibly move abroad, be prepared to be on the move to a different location if he finds out where I live, and consider having a panic room in my home and alarms fitted. Any joint bank accounts or investments that have details of your new current address on their database –. have this removed or highlighted on their system; under no circumstances are your personal details to be given out to Damian or any third party without your knowledge or consent, due to the implications and what can arise as a result. Change career, go to university and re-educate to be able to work in a different field. Get a job – be employed rather than be self-employed, be erased from the records of the electoral roll, and have your national insurance details blocked, don't advertise my business on the Internet or via any form of social media, newspapers, telephone directory or flyers, to be hidden on the list of registrants that governs the professional body that covers the area I work in.

I should relocate my business to another location, and change any mobile numbers, email address, and any other forms of contact, including dissolving any relationships with family/friends as they may expose my whereabouts to Damian. Never have any form of relationship or contact with him or his parents. For every step I take outside, I have to be aware at any point, I am under constant threat of an attack and I must be aware of my surroundings in case I need to escape quickly. It is important to take notice of who is walking behind you, as it could be Damian. Avoid areas that are quiet, stick to busy areas at all times, never be outside alone, always have someone with you. This is how I am expected to live the rest of my life. I should have the right to live without fear and intimidation. I have the right to be me.

How am I expected to run my own business without any form of advertising? To be a ghost of a business that no one has heard of or knows about. Part of the advice is simply unrealistic. I don't fall into the bracket to qualify for help, as I keep being informed, for being self-employed. I am exempt from getting help with further education, housing, legal fees, and also with further police actions. I was advised to take out a non-molestation order at a fee of one thousand and five hundred pounds so they would be able to arrest him if he came within so many miles of me. I feel pressurised to take one out by a domestic abuse support group that works closely with the PPU, but I simply can't afford to. They seem to think that by constantly telling me this is necessary, that this is somehow helping me.

Actually, it's not. I need helpful, practical advice. I don't need to be patronized how I am letting myself down, and what greater risk I am putting myself at for not doing this. I am struggling to make ends meet – I can barely afford to live. I can't afford my legal fees so I have had to take out a loan. Trying to get a loan whilst being hidden on the electoral roll is near impossible, because you are not linked to residing at that property where you now live. You are seen as a negative lender and my solicitors don't do a 'buy now, pay later' plan. It only creates more stress that I could do without. It's a time in your life where you need all the help you can get, I really don't need false promises of help, I would rather not be offered any at all. The cost of the divorce alone is excessive which my solicitor is concerned about. The court will only allow 'reasonable costs', and because it is now so unreasonable, it is unlikely that I will be awarded the full costs back from

117

Damian. The decisions made by the court should have not been allowed to go on for so long. The repetition of submitted evidence, only to go back for further hearings to repeat again, has wasted time, and highly increased my legal fees that should have never mounted to these extreme costs. For every hearing and proposed appeal that he has failed to attend, I have to pay. I am the one funding his time wasting.

They feel they can justify the excessive amount, claiming that by giving him more appeals it is more cost effective. To them, it is. The fear of being personally sued, the only option in protecting themselves is by using, as a shield, a vulnerable woman who has suffered eighteen years of emotional and psychological abuse. If the courts had been firmer with him, I wouldn't be in this situation, paying five times the amount that I should have. I am not the one in control – it's down to the judge's decision, to which I feel the court has taken advantage of. They have already granted another hearing for Damian to attend. They have requested his address for service, and a final decision will be made if he fails to attend.

Due to being bedridden and unable to walk or talk, it was impossible for Damian to attend the fifth appeal. Somehow the letter he had submitted to the court had not arrived to inform them of his absence, but a ten-page detailed dossier managed to get through to the court. He still maintained his ignorance of all the divorce proceedings. He is deeply disturbed by my lack of response to his attack, and to the court's response knowing how ill he is, and after suffering an attack by some criminal, that he has to make an application for an oral appeal, given the state he is in... and the cow jumped over the moon, the little dog laughed, to see such fun, and the dish ran away with the spoon, blah blah blah. To which the court granted him an oral appeal, a further final decision will be made if he fails to attend.

He has no intention of attending this scheduled oral appeal – it's all about manipulating, and controlling the system. Through this, it gives him access to continue his emotional and psychological attacks against me. The court refuses to acknowledge the significance of Damian's ability to attend my workplace and stand outside across the road, staring at me whilst I go in to work. They say it is not an applicable part of the divorce proceedings – confirmation of his address is, and anything else is seen as unimportant as it's not needed. How can it be not needed, when it happened on the day that he was due to appear in court? Neither is it to be taken into account that I have to wear a GPS unit, be on the High Risk register or that the police were called out to come to my workplace for his intimidating behaviour, and that he has an harassment order. They are not interested in the changes I have had to make to my life, trying to protect myself from this man, the constant fear of the threat of being attacked, and the involvement of the PPU.

The schedule date for the sixth appeal was chosen by Damian and the court granted this date, hoping this would solve the mess that had landed in their courthouse for them to sort out. My new instructing barrister is like a bird of prey, ready and waiting, hungry to go in for the attack not only against Damian, but to what has been previously granted with both alternative, and dispense service. This should have never got to this point, mistakes have been made. How can you have faith in the legal system who they have their own agenda, which is what is best for them?

Finally, someone made the decision that should have been made long ago. My decree absolute was granted and posted to the bedbound Damian who failed to attend yet again.

20,160

Fifteen, eight-paged letters sent every week for two years. In total, 20,160 pages I have had to read through to try and trace his whereabouts. He knows I will have to read them, which gives him the opportunity to continue with further emotional and psychological warfare aimed towards me. All cleverly worded to cover the implied threats that may or may not happen to me, all planned to wear me down so I give in to his demands – stop the divorce proceedings and sign over my share of the dungeon to him. He likes to remind me of my childhood and what my father did to me, and writing why wasn't the police called – because I was a whore from an early age, or maybe I was mental like my mother, just making things up like I do now. His friends want revenge for what I have done. They say that I should be taken out into the moors, and be seen to, I need sorting out. Damian always puts up a great defence for me. He likes to point out, to people in the street, that I am not a bad person – he will not hear a bad word said against me. My actions have caused him to have a stroke the doctors have told him, and I should be telling my clients that I am slowly killing him due to my selfishness. He does however worry greatly for my safety, and in great detail describes what it is like where I live, not that he has seen it. You never know when you might get attacked – there are some bad people that do crazy things, especially to women living alone. Why couldn't I have just simply died, it would have made things all the more easier for him. Over ten thousand text messages, one thousand voicemails, one hundred prayer cards and leaflets, and travelling sixty miles three times a week to my place of work to stand and stare or follow me in the streets.

This is not harassment, as I have been informed by numerous police officers who have rolled their eyes in exasperation, sighed, yawned, telling me what they were going to have to eat at their next meal, and made me feel stupid. They accused me of overreacting for reporting this trivial matter, and given me their own interpretation of harassment, which I can recite back, word for word, regarding a famous woman being murdered – that is harassment, and a law was brought out as a result. Not only have I been told I am wasting police time, but also given a lecture of when is the correct time to phone the police. Not when he is standing across the road, ten steps, even four steps away from me, this distance is too far away from me to be considered as threatening. At the point when he places his hand on my body, then I have to wait for him to verbally threaten me – this is the correct time to phone the police, never before, do I understand, nod if I do. I asked the police officer what if he just stabs me without verbally telling me. Apparently, I am missing the point. For it to be harassment, there has to be letters sent every day, and because for three days I don't receive any letters, this is classed as a lengthy period of time without letters so it's not harassment. Text messages aren't taken into account or phone calls unless definite clear threats are made (I am going to kill you, stab you, strangle you). Pamphlets and prayer cards are excluded because they don't have his handwriting on them. Neither does it count that they were sent in an envelope with his handwriting on it.

It is viewed as advertising literature that could have been sent from anywhere, although Catholic monasteries don't usually send out newsletters. There is nothing to connect him to these leaflets. The course he has signed me up to take part in with him is a celebration of a 'perfect marriage', which at the end involves a ceremony in renewing of the marriage vows. Even though this ties in with one of the pamphlets, apparently this is just coincidence and not considered concrete evidence.

When the police officer attended his parents at their home following the failed attempted kidnap, his parents stated they were only trying to bring me back where I belong, and it was only a hammer, there is no real harm in a hammer. They were given a verbal warning, telling them not to do it again. After having to listen to Damian's life story for three hours he admitted he would not stop what he is doing, he is doing it out of love, undying love all for me. All the police officer can say to me is, "Change your mobile number, it's only going to get worse." They have the evidence in front of them and still they do nothing. Apparently it's difficult for the police to get involved, they explained, because of the legal proceedings with the divorce. They tell me it is down to my solicitor for this to be resolved, as I am privately funding my own legal proceedings, and they suggest I further privately fund a civil lawsuit against Damian. In order for this to work I would have to pay for the police's cooperation to enable them to arrest him for his actions. If I don't, there is nothing that can be done – expect the worst.

My solicitor says this is ridiculous, that the police have a duty to be involved with the harassment, regardless of the fact that I am paying for a divorce, and without their involvement there can be no civil lawsuit as the court requires evidence of the police involvement. Where do I go from here? I need help, no one is helping me. I am at a loss where to go to. In desperation, I wrote to the deputy prime minister. I raised my concerns about the difficulties in funding my divorce, and the unrealistic safety issues PPU have recommended, how unclear the law is, which makes the whole divorce process a lengthy one. I feel that the system supports the perpetrator to continue with their behaviour, allowing them to act as freely as they want to, continually allowing them to intimidate. Their life remains the same, whilst you are gathering the pieces from what is left of you, after the wreckage you have struggled to come out of. You are expected to live in fear, and hidden from society in order to protect the perpetrator, and prevent them from attacking or murdering you, this is the police advice, and the success of your survival depends on it. Changes are needed not only in the current laws but also in the legal system, and the police force involvement. It's a time in your life where you need help. A correspondence officer wrote on behalf of the deputy prime minister in response to my letter, stating that government ministers can't get involved in any proceedings nor can they comment to agree, or disagree, and that they are working very hard to raise awareness.

They can confirm that the government had spent forty million pounds to help domestic abuse organisations. They quoted the Matrimonial Causes Act 1973, and explained about Legal Services Commission (LSC) that relates to legal aid, which takes into account income state benefits, including housing benefit, local housing allowance, council tax benefit, independent living fund payments and disability living allowance. They hope this information is helpful. It is not helpful at all. I am relaying my experience, as a woman living and contributing to this country's growth, the difficulties I am currently experiencing to a member of parliament within our government. A government is there to implement changes to our country that affects everyone who lives here, including education, forming new laws, and health – our lives are governed by this political party. To be able to do this and enable change, information has to be gathered from people's experiences, and the action of the authorities involved. Lying on a pillow then pulling it over your ears, and closing your eyes isn't going to make something go away. Your value as a citizen is only recognised every four years, when they want your golden ticket that you possess, your vote.

My silence and zero response to Damian's relentless terror campaign only fuels him more. In his letters, he actually writes as if I have written back to him, fuelling his frenzied allegations against me. The evidence of my sins is written there in the Bible. He will do whatever the Lord Almighty instructs him to do. It's not because he wants to, it is how it is, and how it has to be. No matter how many brick walls I put up to stop, and block him contacting me, he finds a way, and knocks the wall down to get to me. The more I move away, the more he keeps moving forward; he keeps tapping away to make his presence ever felt, he is not going to let me go, and no matter what I do he will track me down. To find out my new address, he reported me to the police stating I have stolen his bank account card, referring to a joint bank account, which was opened in order to pay the monthly mortgage payments. He went into the bank demanding a full explanation, and their actions have resulted in the police's involvement in this theft. The bank's failings are that they had breached a confidentiality clause. He had not received his new card that they routinely send through the post every two years. He threatened to sue them, claiming they had sent it to a wrong address and quoting a few legal acts is a sure way to get what he wants from the bank that likes to give you that extra help. To get rid of the problem presenting itself in front of them, which is persisting and persisting, not only did they do what he wanted but also provided Damian with a print-off, containing details of my name and address.

If the bank assistant had firstly checked the record of transactions details in the joint bank account, to see how payments have been made into the account, they would have seen that Damian made cheque payments into the joint bank account via the cash machine and, to do this, he would have had to use his card. So how can it be stolen? And what thief would pay money into a bank account? The dirty secret, which Damian suggested to my solicitor, should be kept between the two of them, is that the court does not need to be notified that he knows about my whereabouts. To prove he knew, he enclosed a copy of the print-off the bank gave him. Referring to the court is relating to me, this alarmed my solicitor and they contacted me to warn me of the breach that had occurred within the bank, and that my safety was a greater issue. I had been reassured some four months ago by a bank assistant that they would never pass my details onto Damian – they made a note on the bank's computer system never to do so. This would flash up on the screen if any bank assistant went into the system, and logged into the joint bank account details. Given the circumstances, and on the advice of the PPU, I took a letter directly into the bank explaining the situation. I emphasised why they must never pass any of my personal details onto Damian, as they will be putting my safety at even greater risk if he finds out the location of my address. I even showed them the GPS unit I was wearing. At first the bank admitted liability in branch when I presented them my letter of complaint, and a copy of the print-off which had the bank's branch stamp on with the date on when this was issued.

I was assured by the member of staff at the bank that my letter was going to be forwarded directly to head office for investigation. Four weeks has passed, and still no response. It was only when I contacted the financial ombudsmen that they finally made contact, seven weeks later, stating that they had no knowledge of this occurrence. The letter I had previously taken into the bank has mysteriously been deleted, with no trace of it existing at all. Neither could any staff members in the bank remember ever having a conversation with myself relating to this. For something that they deny has happened, I find it rather odd, when I walk into the bank, that the bank assistant on the information desk always looks at me sheepishly and hurtles off at such speed towards a room at the back inside the bank. They return in tow with a supervisor or manager, heading in my direction only to harass me and bombard me with a constant repeated statement "everything is all right now, everything is all right now, everything is all right now, everything is all right now." Do they feel by repeating this statement, as many times as possible in my face, that it will brainwash me into dropping my complaint. In order to understand my complaint to effectively deal with it, I was subjected to a horrendous telephone interview. Feeling very vulnerable, I felt I was taken advantage of due to the situation by being asked extremely difficult questions: when was I last attacked, the likelihood of when I will be next attacked, to give an approximate timescale, in days or weeks, when the next attack will happen, and how do I think what the end result of the attack will be?

In between the questions, I was constantly placed on hold, while the customer service adviser goes to speak to their supervisor, to return back with more questions. This went on for forty minutes, after which I was informed by the customer service advisor that, with immediate effect, they were placing a block on the joint bank – no money can go in or out due to the situation. I would not be in this situation, or having this conversation with them, if they had not given Damian my details. I had to beg this customer service advisor not to take this action – it will cause a missed payment on the mortgage payment that is due out that very same day. There isn't time to prevent this, even though all I am asking is for them to allow the mortgage payment to go through, then block the account. The customer service advisor is pressurising me to take the compensation offer that has now increased to three hundred and fifty pounds, for the distress and inconvenience, and to close the complaint. Nothing else can be done, the account is being blocked. Again, they would like to offer three hundred and fifty pounds to help resolve this situation – "It might help with unexpected costs." This is being treated fairly – my complaint being resolved is to be blackmailed into accepting this offer or else they are blocking the account. I declined. I ended up paying the mortgage payment on my credit card to avoid any penalties with the account being blocked. I cannot believe how the bank has tried to cover up their mistakes, by sending me a letter the next day from the customer service advisor.

They note I feel they have breached confidentiality and, having reviewed the account, this isn't the case. The bank did not breach data protection due to it being a joint bank account, and both account holders are entitled to any information they hold. They confirm that no block has been placed on the account, even though they have advised me it should be blocked. By not blocking the account it means that myself, and Damian are liable for this to occur again. If it had been blocked, none of this would have happened. The amount has been increased to five hundred pounds – they are very keen to resolve the complaint, and for the payment to be issued. I declined this offer as I feel the bank's dishonest intentions are far from satisfactory. As far as the financial ombudsmen are concerned, it has been resolved – the bank has satisfactorily proved they have explained the situation, and tried to make things right. The only other alternative is to fund my own legal case against the bank, but, as an advising solicitor pointed out, seeing how I am not suffering, because I am managing to work, and have not turned to alcohol or drugs, it's harder to prove to the court that the impact of this has had any significance on my life. How could they possibly compensate me, because I haven't lost anything through this? How ridiculous is that based on those three factors? I have no option to carry on working, social security are not going to help me, so what other option do I have? I have never taken drugs nor have I ever had an issue with alcohol.

I choose not to drink alcohol, because I feel inside that if I did, I know I wouldn't stop. It's not going to alter the situation – the problem will still remain the same, and I would have a head from hell. It's not the path I am going to take. I am having counselling to cope, so I am able to function, and to go to work. The bank has created more stress – the nightmares increased and I need more counselling, which I am privately funding. Even more worrying, they have put my safety at greater risk, both now and in the future. All PPU can do is put me in contact with a group that deals in panic rooms, that I should consider having one installed in my home. The leaflet that I have been sent explains how it works, with a phone installed in a designated room that links direct to the police, with metal bars fixed across the window on the outside, and a metal grill covering the door. I find this unbearable – it is going to make me feel like I am back living in the dungeon. The personal alarm he made me wear has been replaced with a GPS unit. I feel trapped, I am not free. Not only has he managed to orchestrate the police in maintaining his control over me – by keeping me in the life he feels I should have – but I have no life at all, imprisoned inside and fearful from the outside world.

It's easier for me to accommodate Damian's actions, seeing how a police officer remarked, "it's like pissing in the wind talking to him." They haven't the time or energy to deal with him, and he knows this.

Refusing to answer the door at the dungeon killed two birds with one stone – he didn't have to explain his behaviour, or get a cautionary warning from the attending police officer who, after several failed attempts, got bored and no further action was taken. My reported incident got shelved to gather dust. The easiest way for the police to deal with this is through me – by keeping the fear instilled, and treating me no different to how I have been treated my entire life, piling on the guilt, and instructing me to do as I am told to, for I am far easier to be controlled. They treat me with the contempt I deserve and communicate to me in the only way I have been accustomed, as they seem to think this is the only way I can understand – talking to me with a raised voice, loud enough that anyone standing three hundred metres away would hear, slow enough so I can understand the spoken words from the police officers mouths, to reiterate only what they have said several times before. They constantly refer to the need to create picture of the situation before they can consider if police involvement is necessary. Building a story from the reported events that have occurred gives them a greater insight into the situation between Damian and myself. The countless times I have reported the letters to the police and spent many an evening sitting in a cold police station after work whilst two police officers read through his comments written in the letter, trying to decipher if the implied threats are deemed as threatening enough to take action. This picture that has been growing and growing for the last two years.

It is not enough that a chief inspector been contacted directly by my solicitor regarding the implied threat towards me, and informing them that I have been issued with a GPS unit and given safety procedures from the police protection unit, as they are so alarmed by his actions that they felt it necessary to warn me about my imminent death and that he will be the one murdering me. I find it hard to believe when the police say there is not enough evidence presented to them, based on the data they have on record, it does not warrant any further action against Damian, as the picture is unclear. They insist that I must keep reporting every incident that occurs no matter how trivial, as it could be the vital piece of information they need to nail the bastard. This plausible excuse they keep giving me every time, and every time I report something in the hope that this will be the time they actually do something, only to be told "not this time, maybe next." On the basis of a theory of a very experienced police officer, so experienced they felt the need to inform me of this great wealth of experience they possessed – having dealt with these matters involving people like me: aka (also known as) a police time-waster, a domestic – defined as an overreacting woman who sniffs the daisies, is away with the fairies, sat drinking cat pee whilst talking to the clouds about a pile of drivel, complaining about her ex-husband who acts like a scorned adolescent woman, with a mild fixation on his ex-wife. He will soon get over it; case closed. They deduced that I wasn't at any great threat from Damian, and there is no real cause for concern.

Denying there is no crime reduces crime. If you tell everyone the number of burglaries was higher last year, it will increase it, as it will make people want to become a burglar –

it is seen as an advertisement, and so it encourages more people to do this. So that is why Damian does what he does, because of an advert. He is not held accountable for his actions or is responsible in any way whatsoever for sending a constant barrage of text messages that fills my entire memory space in my phone, or for the fact that no one can call me as the phone is constantly engaged due to the volume of messages he, and his mother are leaving day and night. Denying this is happening isn't going to stop it – if anything, it is getting worse.

A hairdresser and close friend of Damian's mother was more than happy to help get my new mobile number for her friend, by obtaining it from one of her clients. Somehow the hairdresser had misplaced my mobile number, desperate to get hold of me as she was in absolute agony with her toe, and my client being the kind person they are, gladly gave the hairdresser my new number.

This has greatly impacted on my work, because I have had to change my mobile number five times, to prevent this hairdresser from continually passing my number onto Damian's mother so she, and her son, can continue with the intensity of the harassment which they constantly work so hard at. I have had no option but to stop treating clients that go to this hairdresser, and any clients that are connected through being a friend or relative of clients who visit this hairdresser.

I can no longer work within a six-mile radius of where his parents live due to his father, who has taken it upon himself to car-patrol this area in military-style, complete with a combat knife and wooden baseball bat, in preparation for when he sees my car and can slash all of my tyres… and possibly me too.

They are passing the buck, claiming it is not the responsibility of the police to intervene. Then whose is it? No one's, it seems. It is acceptable that I have to live in fear, and accommodate continued emotional and psychological abuse, to be prepared to pack up and leave at a moment's notice and run, whenever he comes into my area. But where to? Probably the ends of the earth, because this man is relentless – he isn't giving up and neither are his parents. This is the solution to the problem, according to the police. They also advised me not to aggravate him, as it might make him commit a crime, which he may later regret, and could I bear being held responsible? For it can only be one person's fault. Dangle me out as bait long enough to see what happens – what a great experiment in putting Damian to the test. In fact, I think it is the other way round – Damian proving not only can he come and go as he pleases, but also that there is nothing the police will do to help me, and he knows this. The police constantly dismiss his ability and the depth of his legal knowledge, which he uses to his advantage.

All perfectly planned and timed to perfection, as always – he knew full well the estimated time of arrival of the police, what with traffic at a busy period of the day, will give him at least an hour, maybe a little less, to play sick mind games from the moment I have dialled 999 and explained why I have called. He probably knows the content of the conversation, when I say to the operator he is standing across the road staring. "What, not on the premises?" "No, he is standing across the road." "Why is he doing that?" "He is intimidating me." "What makes you think he is doing that, and what do you want the police to do?"

134

I explain about wearing a GPS unit and the involvement of the PPU, who have applied a tag on my work's premises, which flashes up that a blue light response is required with an estimated time of arrival of twenty minutes when this address is given. Apparently not. The operator informed me that there was no tag to warrant such a response – the police will be with you shortly. Stay inside the building, and lock all doors and windows. While the clinic went into lock down mode, I treated my client and then contacted my solicitor to inform them what was happening, as Damian was still claiming to the courts that he is bedridden. The solicitor asked if I could get a photo of him, but this was impossible due to a whopping great oak tree in the way. Then they suggested I ask the receptionist to go out and do it. Hardly! I would never ask anyone to do something that I wouldn't be prepared to do myself and, hand on heart, I cannot say that he would not attack them. I could not put anyone at that risk. The police came one hour and thirty minutes later, followed with a fifteen minute discussion with the attending police officers to assess the situation.

After looking up and down the road, they finally decided the next best course of action was to check behind all the surrounding dustbins, but to no avail. They could not find Damian, and, with at least four walking escape routes, regular points to access public transport and a main road to get quickly into a car, it wasn't rocket science that he would not be there. How certain was I that he was there? Two witnesses, that's how certain. The police couldn't write this incident off, and had no option but to issue Damian with a harassment order. If he continues in what he is doing, then they will take further action against him.

Two months after this incident, the PPU decided I was no longer at high risk – the time had come to return to them the GPS unit. I was only too glad to for it to go, as it was gathering dust in my cupboard. It was no use to me. I made the decision and stopped wearing it soon after the incident, and finally came to terms with what will be, will be. For this little box with a flashing light was not going to protect me, and neither are the police going to come in time to help me.

No longer will I constantly look over my shoulder, open another urgent 'read me' letter, I will walk as slow, or as fast as I can, jump hop or skip, look up to the sky or at my feet. When I handed over this little box assuming it will be handed to another person to wear, I was told it's probably not working as a lot of them don't.

The purpose of this little box was solely for the protection of the police, should they ever be questioned on what they had done to protect me from the man whom they knew to be intent on killing me. Litigation – this is all it ever comes down to. I have tried my best, I can do no more. All I have done is ask for help, only to have doors closed, and walls built against me. I thought the police were there to help you. How wrong was I!

The sick bird hit, by man at sea.

A date has been listed for the next court hearing – the start of the financial dispute resolution or FDR. There will be a total of three appointments or court hearings – the first and second appointments, and then a final hearing – all to finalise who gets what from the assets, savings, pensions, belongings and equity from the former matrimonial home, and anything else that you have a joint share of. A 'Form E' has to be filled in by both parties, a detailed dossier which ends up being the thickness of a 1980s telephone directory, where you have to submit one year's bank statements from all bank accounts, including any accounts that you have closed, pension forecast (what you're likely to get when you retire) from any private pension, and including state pension, the approximate current market value of the former matrimonial home, the remaining balance of the outstanding mortgage, which has to be confirmed with a mortgage redemption certificate from the bank, and, finally, all of your weekly and monthly income and outgoings. No stone is left unturned. This builds a picture of your financial situation from how much you spend on clothes, haircuts, sanitary products, and the cost of that cup of coffee you buy when you go out. Your financial details are all completely scrutinised by each other's solicitors and you have to justify that is a necessary part of your living expenses, even down to why you buy a packet of mints, and any monies you have withdrawn from your bank account. A full explanation is required to explain why you have done this, and evidence is needed to where it went, and receipts to confirm this.

All of this has to be submitted to the court, which takes into account various considerations on what order should be made. In other words, who gets what. The court considers all aspects. Firstly, the welfare of any children in the family under the age of eighteen years of age. Then they look at your income and your potential earning capacity for the foreseeable future, any property or other financial resources that you have, or will be likely have in the future – the court's opinion of what they expect you to acquire. They also take into account any financial needs, obligations, and responsibilities that you have or are likely to have in the future, as well as the contributions made or likely to make in the foreseeable future to the welfare of the family, including any contribution made by looking after the family home or caring for the family. In addition, they look at what age you entered the marriage, and the standard of living before the breakdown of the marriage, any mental or physical disability that either of you have, and if the conduct of either of you is unacceptable to the degree that, in the court's opinion, would be unfair to disregard. Finally, the value of you. Due to the divorce, will you lose the chance of acquiring property and pensions? The court trusts that you will have an absolute duty to each other during the FDR proceedings, that you will fully disclose your financial position so that a fair financial arrangement can be made. Failing to do so, in that you have been deliberately untruthful, might result in criminal proceedings being brought against you under the Fraud Act 2006. Your signed statement of truth declares that, if any false statement is found, then proceedings for contempt of court may be brought against you.

You are given three months to fill in, complete, and submit the Form E to each other's solicitor, and to the court ready for the scheduled hearing. My solicitor was contacted by several solicitors from different law firms, all of which had refused to represent Damian after it became apparent during the initial consultation with him, his difficult, and unreasonable behaviour. With no one representing him, he may well do it himself. This in itself could present problems, in which he could delay matters further, by using his ill health as grounds. Trying to get a response from him, as my solicitor has found, is like trying to get blood out of a stone – he completely ignores any letters that are sent to him regarding the proceedings, and with the hearing for the FDR fast approaching, he still has yet to get legal representation, which my solicitor is urging him to do. Three months of waiting, feels like it is just prolonging the endless mind torture. I want this to be over, there has to be an end to this.

Finally, the time has come; time to face my fears.

"Is this genuine?" district judge three asked, wafting a letter in the air that had been submitted fifteen minutes before the hearing. It was handwritten on a plain piece of paper, with the date and time of a medical appointment booked at the hospital. Normally hospitals send your appointments through the post on letter headed paper, with all the details of your appointment typed. This hand written medical appointment was not the only reason why Damian was not attending the first FDR hearing.

His legal representative is not able to write a letter or contact the court on his behalf, which he knows full well; without the public funding certificate, they are not going to start any work. Damian has a dispute going on with the legal aid contributions – he is insisting that he does not have to pay any contributions towards his legal fees – as he is on state benefits, he is exempt. District judge three remarked that they are fully aware of Damian's capacity with his legal knowledge, and that he has had time to obtain legal representation for the scheduled hearing. He should have paid the contribution then appealed the decision afterwards. The Form E is a straightforward document, that he is more than competent to complete, as he is capable of writing lengthy letters to the court, and that despite his alleged health problems, he seems to have the energy and time to write these letters. It was then that district judge three ordered that Damian has fourteen days to submit his Form E, medical report, and confirmation from the hospital that he did attend the medical appointment on the day of the hearing. As a result of this failed attempt at a first FDR hearing, it has been adjourned. The next scheduled date and time has yet to be confirmed when the next first FDR hearing will take place.

Having an harassment order issued is a bit of a hindrance to Damian but there are other ways he can get his messages through to me.

The sinister accusations of what might or might not happen have to go – it has become too much of a risk to expose himself. Alternatively, he can use the court who will be unknowingly delivering his messages for him. The court has a duty to duplicate and pass on to my solicitor whatever he sends to them in relation to the hearings. He uses this as a cover to continue his harassment.

A typed letter from a person claiming to be a friend of Damian's, who has no legal experience, wants it to be known that Damian is still waiting for a response from the legal service commissions in relation to the public funding certificate, and will be seeking advice from his solicitor. Damian has no experience in this area of law, therefore no presumptions should be made in relation to the Form E – it will be sent with the court's specifications, and his GP has forwarded the medical report to the court. Decoded, this translates as he may or may not get in contact with the legal commissions, he might not be at the court hearing, he has yet to decide who is going to be his solicitor, and he shouldn't be expected to fill in this Form E as it is beneath him. There are numerous specifications relating to the Form E, for example the colour of the paper it should be on, what colour ink to fill it in with, what information he chooses to disclose, and it has to be typed up by the solicitor's secretary before it can be submitted to the court and so on. He will decide, not the court, which specification he feels appropriate in these circumstances. He has no intention whatsoever of contacting his GP – he has better things to do with his time.

He knows this will be forwarded on to my solicitor and that my solicitor has a duty of care to inform me of this information. There is no escaping his messages – he knows they will get through either verbally or sent through to me in the post. What am I going to do? Complain to the police that the court and my solicitor are sending me post I don't want to receive? It is all in relation to the current FDR hearings I am instigating against my ex-husband and it just makes me look like a crazy person. To anyone reading this without any knowledge of Damian, there is no malicious intent.

The court has listed a date for the next attempt at a first FDR appointment with district judge three sitting at the hearing. There is no getting out of this hearing – the court order has made it very clear that they require his Form E before the hearing, and that if he fails to attend without good reason, they will make a final order on the day. In regards to what I am seeking as a settlement from the marriage, it is not huge. I don't want his pension or savings or shares that he has. I don't want any of the furniture, carpets, curtains or fixtures and fittings from the dungeon, or the pots, pans and cutlery that I have bought – he can keep the whole lot. Seeing how I have paid fifty percent of the mortgage, plus my contribution into continually maintaining the dungeon inside and out over the years, I feel I am entitled to fifty percent of the dungeon, which has to be sold or he buys me out so he can continue living there. Plus I am seeking full costs from him in relation to the divorce proceedings, to be paid from his fifty percent share of the dungeon. With there being no children involved, it is quite simple in what we are asking the court.

A performance worthy of an acting award, being pushed in a wheelchair by his father into the court building, with his mother wiping the tears from her eyes as she briskly walks at the side of her son. Sat slumped to one side, head hanging down, eyes closed, with his mouth open and saliva oozing from it, jaw protruding to a jaunty angle, hands held in a rigid foetal position, and his ankles securely strapped to the wheelchair to prevent him from slipping out, and onto the floor during the bouts of fitting seizures followed by unconsciousness, entered Damian. This grand entrance has definitely convinced the court security guards, bantering with each other and trying to figure out what has happened, whilst one of them body searched me and the other checked through my handbag for dangerous weapons that I might be trying to bring in to the court building. Both of them came to the decision that he had been in a car crash – of course, that's why he was at court – for compensation. Surely no one would be sick enough to make a severely disabled person in that state go to court, no one could be that cruel. I must be cruel, and that is exactly what Damian wants to portray to the court. How could I do this to this poor man, and abandon him, given the state he is in? What chance do I have in court with this act? He is so hell bent on giving this performance, and with the help of his parents. Also self-medicating with at least one weeks course, from his chest of drawers that houses his own private drug collection. On a legal level it is purely all above board, because it is all entirely prescribed by his doctor, unaware of Damian's intentions.

Damian tests and records the medication given to him, depending on what symptoms he tells his doctor he has, by noting what the outcome of the prescribed drug he has taken, and the side effects it has on him. He keeps a detailed log, how many days to take, including the dosage, which he will alter depending how much of an impact he needs to have. If it means overdosing, he will do this. What situation he needs it for can be anything – to have extra time off from work, as thirty-two days holiday entitlement isn't enough. Depending how long he feels is necessary to have off from work, he can choose from the desired outcome from the side effects whether it is flu symptoms, jaundice, sickness, or diarrhoea.

He can recreate anything from his collection, including stroke-like symptoms: headaches, confusion, slurred speech, unbalanced coordination combined with numbness in the limbs and tingling sensations. Prescribed insomnia medication has a multitude of benefits, and when taken at the right time presents you with a state of unconsciousness. Combined with his mother's amateur dramatics, demanding she has to be with her son at all times of the day, to wipe the dribble from his mouth, and insisting she has to be allowed into the hearing to do this. In addition, being in an unfamiliar room all alone could trigger off one of his fitting seizures, so she has to be on hand to assist him. Together, they have set the scene.

However, his mother's demands were rebuked by district judge three on the grounds that it is a court hearing, which neither of them are entitled to attend nor does it require them to be in the hearing. They would have to make do with sitting on the toughened plastic bench bolted into the ground, in the private waiting area in the corridor directly outside the courtroom, whilst their son attends the court hearing with his instructing solicitor.

No one can access these corridors. If you are attending the court for a hearing, everyone has to be in the main waiting area under the watchful eye of the security guards, until you are called by the court usher – only then will you gain access through the corridor. The entrance doors to the corridors all have a keypad lock attached to the door and the court usher enters the access code to unlock the door through into the narrow corridor with its sharp square corners. It is like being in a maze, except there are no hedges or sky above your head, the only light that there is coming in is from the fluorescent tubes built into the sloping ceiling with the industrial concrete walls. When the door closes shut, it automatically locks everyone inside the corridor. The private waiting area in the corridor is used when the district judge needs time for recess during the hearing – you all have to vacate the courtroom and go into the corridor, and wait here until you are all ushered back into the court room for the hearing to continue, to hear the district judge's final decision.

Trying to reduce the stress of the hearing, my solicitor not only arranged with the district judge three that if I found it too difficult being in the same room as Damian, I could leave the courtroom at any point during the hearing, but also arranged with the court usher that we could enter the courtroom first. This means I didn't have to endure being locked in the confined space with Damian or his parents, or having to walk through with them down the narrow corridor to the court room. This enabled me to position my chair so I was facing my solicitor and the district judge three. Before Damian came into the courtroom my solicitor warned me there may be a possibility that Damian might have a seizure during the hearing – apparently he has at least eight a day, and that he keeps going in and out of unconsciousness. In the event of this happening his father will be asked to take Damian out of the courtroom and the hearing will continue without him.

Damian entered the room, wheeled in by his father, and was placed at the farthest point on the conference table away from me, completely out of my sight. My solicitor, and district judge three together rolled their eyes at Damian's father's performance, who gave his unconscious son a kiss on his forehead, telling him they are just outside so he must tell his solicitor if he needs them. Due to Damian's disability, his solicitor says he is entitled to more than fifty percent of the dungeon. Because of his extensive disabilities, and rapidly deteriorating health, both of his parents are now his full-time carers.

He is unable to ever go back into employment as a result of being stabbed. The attack has left him wheelchair bound due to the nerve damage in his spine, and the stroke he has suffered means he can no longer speak – the only way he can communicate is through a series of grunts. Therefore he does not have the capacity to have a mortgage, which is why he requires a greater share of the dungeon – to be precise, eighty-five percent of the dungeon would enable him to purchase a bungalow and have no mortgage. He relies on money given to him through claiming state benefits and the disability living allowance. Damian is also entitled to a further nine thousand pounds – his solicitor produced in court a copy of a signed deed, containing what looked like my signature, saying that I agree, in the event of the dungeon ever being sold, he would be entitled to the first nine thousand pounds from the sale. Both mine and Damian's signatures were witnessed by one of his work colleagues.

This deed was updated, and transformed six years later, a week prior to getting married, to a pre-nuptial agreement – in the event that we separated or divorced, the dungeon was to be sold and I agreed to forfeit to Damian nine thousand pounds. Both signatures were witnessed by another work colleague. This is the first time I have heard of these contracts, and seen them in court. Can he really do this? District judge three is not convinced these are genuine. It makes me doubt them myself, but when I look at my signature, it looks identical to mine. The consent form Damian had me signing, requesting him to be my instructing solicitor for the road traffic accident I was involved in, was the last form I have signed. He brought home to the dungeon the documents for me to sign in front of him.

Due to this, it was difficult to prove otherwise – with the forms being properly executed, there was nothing that could be done about this. Damian is entitled to the first nine thousand pounds from the sale of the dungeon. As for the eighty-five percent, Damian's solicitor is insisting that it is rightfully his on the grounds of ill health, but district judge three is not so convinced due to the lack of information that has been provided to the court. Why are his needs so different that he requires more than fifty percent? No medical report has been submitted to the court from his practising GP, which the court ordered seven days prior to the hearing. The submitted Form E is incorrectly filled in and is not to the court's specifications, as it is all handwritten by Damian's mother, with repeated spelling mistakes, crossings out, and written comments like 'don't know, you will have to find it out yourselves' underlined with multiple exclamation marks, and a failure to disclose bank statements.

This is clearly delaying matters, not to mention the colossal costs that have been incurred as a result. This telling off falls entirely on the shoulders of Damian's solicitor, whom district judge three is more than happy to remind them that they are aware of the court proceedings, are they not? If their client does not stop, and continues to write to the court with these lengthy letters, this will increase his costs. "Furthermore, I know you understand," district judge three says, directly challenging Damian about his drugged-up act, particularly when money is mentioned, for then Damian becomes more alert to the hearing. His performance is fooling no one.

His solicitor has to once more bear the brunt of their client's actions as they are given another dressing down in court; that they need to be firmer and make sure their client adheres to the rules of the court. These orders are to be adhered to for the next hearing; he has fourteen days in which to submit the fully completed Form E to the court, along with the identity of the medical expert who is required to do a report on Damian. The hearing has been adjourned to another first appointment. All questionnaires relating to each other's Form E have to be submitted to the court, and each other's solicitors one month before the next scheduled hearing.

It's my problem the joint bank account is frozen, Damian accepts no liability – this was all brought on by my laziness. His solicitor added that it is about time I started being cooperative during the hearings and to make an effort to resolve this, and not make it any more difficult than it has to be. Their sick client does not trust me and under no circumstances will they give their bank account details, so I had better pull my finger out in sorting this situation.

Whilst waiting for your hearing to be called, both solicitors go to a quiet area in the court building, and they do an engagement of conversation, whereby they each discuss what you are wanting and report back to you with the deal they are offering. If you choose to accept then you don't have to go into the court hearing as you have settled out of court; if not, you continue and go ahead with the court hearing for the district judge to decide.

Damian's solicitor feels the need to resort to underhand tactics and uses this as prime time to tell of their woeful work problems, highlighting this very trying period that they are currently experiencing in the hope that it might help in resolving the situation. In light of this, my solicitor says we should feel sorry for them, and be understanding as they have the misfortune of having such a difficult client. All jobs have a certain amount of difficulties, it is the nature of them; if you don't like fires, you don't become a fire fighter, expecting to rescue cats all day long who are stuck up a trees – the chances of you being a fire fighter, and never having to attend a house fire is zero, it's going to happen. The plight of Damian's solicitor's needs is the deal, not exactly what I was expecting, this plea of desperation all done behind closed doors. Damian's solicitor is very ambitious, with a stream of awards presented to them, and so early on in their career. They have their own agenda, with a record of very successfully completed cases that they have represented – they are not going to want to lose this one and have a blot on their perfect record. Clearly they are very resourceful in thinking of ways to try and quickly tie up this case which is proving to be more difficult than they anticipated.

It is not my concern that they are having difficulties at work with their client, who deliberately monopolises all of their time by constantly bombarding them with letters, and phone calls with daily direct instructions they must obey. All draft copies of letters that Damian has compiled, and issued to his solicitor, whom he treats as a secretary, must use the exact wording and contents, even down to the last full stop; nothing is to be changed without his direct consent. The allocated hours paid under the legal funding have been quickly exhausted to the point that the work on his case has come to an abrupt halt, until more coins are paid into the law firm's meter. Work on his case will be resumed once they are in receipt of the certificate of funding provided by the legal aid commissions. Damian has to reapply by providing evidence to them, confirming his financial position has not changed since he last applied in order to qualify. Will he or won't he do this is anyone's guess. With no one at the helm to steer the ship that is veering off in all directions, all chaos breaks out. Being off the radar, and refusing to acknowledge any emails or phone calls for three weeks raises concerns, with the scheduled court hearing growing nearer and still there is no response from Damian's solicitor to indicate whether or not they have found a medical expert – if they have not, my solicitor has found three, and already has their CVs to hand and price estimates for them to approve one of them prior to the hearing. Here lies the problem – since Damian's entire case is built around his health issues, without a medical report we are unable to proceed with the FDR, as it will be difficult for the district judge to make a fair decision.

There are many questions I have in relation to his alleged health claims, and his Form E. If he is so ill as he is claiming to be, then why hasn't he informed the insurance firm, which we pay a premium to every month for mortgage protection. This covers us both in the event of having a stroke, terminal illness, or one of thirty other various health conditions they deem as serious enough, they will pay the remaining balance of your mortgage off, so you don't have the added pressure of losing your home, and becoming homeless. How many times a week does he go to the hospital to see the specialist consultant, and how does he travel there. Can he confirm on a daily basis, how much assistance he has from his parents to help him, and in what capacity. Feeding, dressing, bathing, going to the toilet, help getting in and out of bed, preparing meals, and are they part or full-time carers. Why does he not live with his parents, wouldn't it be easier for them to be at the same property for his care needs, rather than having to travel to this sizeable property that he requires to live in. If he is too ill to work, how has he managed to have written, and published four books about religion, and self-promote himself by going on a world tour with his agent. Does he intend to have more books published, how much revenue was made on the book sales, and what was his net income after business expenses. Has he declared the money earned to the Inland Revenue Services, or informed social services about the money he has been paid whilst claiming state benefits, under the pretence of not being able to work on the grounds of his failing health which prevents him from being employed.

What has happened to his shares that he has, and the three bank accounts that he uses for savings – there is no mention of them, or the three private pensions he has paid into. Can he confirm if someone else is holding his money in another bank account, and if so can he disclose their full name and all details including amount in the account, deposits made, and the location of the bank account. When the dungeon was purchased, can he acknowledge that I spent eighteen thousand pounds, which was used to purchase all the furnishings, and renovating throughout the entire property; his nine thousand pounds was used as a deposit to purchase the dungeon. Finally, about this huge financial debt of an unknown sum that he owes to his parents, is a result of not being able to pay the mortgage, and various other bills. He cannot say what the exact amount is, for his parents didn't keep a record of the money they have given him since I left him. It is up to the district judge to what they see fit, given the circumstances, what would be an appropriate amount to give them from the sale of the dungeon – of course, he is not implying that it should come from my share of the property.

His solicitor likes to over-emphasise how reasonable their client is, as he has agreed to pay my divorce costs. Given the chance he would like to pay it now, but at present with money being a bit tight, living on the poverty line, having mere bread and water to survive, he simply hasn't the pennies to give me all ten thousand pounds. This will be eventually paid out of his share, from the proceeds of the sale of the dungeon.

Under no circumstances is their client trying to delay matters by avoiding answering these questions. It is simply an oversight on their part entirely, and in view of such they will not be ready for the next scheduled FDR hearing. They have made an application to the court requesting the FDR to be further adjourned to another date, by which time they will have the medical report ready to submit to court. Further to this, my actions are questionable, and have been drawn to the court's attention which has added to the delay of the FDR hearing. They would like to point out that I have purposely hidden from the court, by excluding on my submitted Form E, a property that I own; this should be taken into account for the financial settlement. They use this information to cover their own actions, having failed to inform the court that the medical expert who was going to perform the medical report, had discharged him from under their care at the hospital some time ago. A minor oversight – there is no consultant to perform the medical report. Why is there no consultant at present? Because Damian isn't as ill as he is making out to be. Why else would he be discharged, other than because there is nothing there to treat? They distract the court by drawing the focus of attention back to me, in a desperate bid to recover the aftermath of what their client has created. In light of this information, are we agreeable to the hearing being adjourned? The time period they are looking at is two months for the next scheduled FDR hearing. This is due to their client's limited availability for the next month, as he will be attending various hospital appointments everyday for treatment, and for the following month no one will be available to bring their client to the court.

May I be reminded of the consequences of failing to disclose all information relating to the financial proceedings? This period of time will give me the opportunity to reflect and to gather all the relevant evidence they require – confirmation of ownership of the said property, mortgage capacity based on my earnings, what size property and where I intend to live, all to be submitted to them and the court before the hearing.

There is no level Damian or his solicitor won't sink to, for this property is someone's home – it is my mother's home, and it has been since she left my father over twenty years ago and went there to live with her brother shortly before he died. During her divorce, a deed of trust (which allows my mother to live in the property until her death) was placed on my deceased uncle's property. This prevented my father from making a financial claim on the property, which would have resulted in the property being sold and my mother being made homeless. In order to prevent this, a deed of trust was drawn up with two other named trustees associated with the property – my sister and I. Being a shareholder meant mother's share was small enough so father couldn't make a claim, and that my sister and I equally inherit her share of the property only in the event of mother's death. Only then can it be sold, and the proceeds of the sale to be equally divided between the two of us. Based on this, there was no reason to include this on my Form E.

My solicitor pointed out that future inheritance is not considered to be part of the financial settlement, and reassured me there wasn't any real cause for concern, with it being my mother's home for such a length of time, and in reality there was nothing Damian can do about this. In light of these allegations my solicitor felt it was wise before the next hearing to contact the land register for confirmation of ownership, which confirmed that I owned a third of the property along with my mother and sister. The key to knowing about my involvement with the property is through the deed of trust, which my solicitor needs to have access to. For this, consent is required from my mother and sister who I haven't seen or spoken to in years. Knowing full well the pain of being rejected by my own mother and how deeply this hurt me, Damian was on the front row seat observing the full impact it had on me. By placing me back into that same situation, he knows full well how difficult it is going to be for me to contact my mother. After witnessing the last spoken words I said to her, "you will never hear from me or see me again." For the first time in my life to turn to her, and ask her for her help that I need. Would she help, or possibly reject me for a second time? How would that feel? Would it hurt as much as it did the first time or would it hurt more? It has to be the latter – with no doubt, and what better way to ensure this will happen Damian sent my mother a letter to inform her of the wicked actions of her younger daughter, who is just like her father, trying to evict him from the marital home. Given his present condition, having suffered a stroke which has made him weak, and afraid of what I might do next, he felt she should be made aware of my actions.

By creating this picture, Damian has set the scene by reintroducing my mother's own fears of possibly becoming homeless, playing on history repeating itself, except her ex-husband is no longer the enemy, her younger daughter is. I am damned if I contact her, as it is clear what my intentions are, which isn't for a big family reunion, it is just to access the deed, which understandably opens up the question, what am I intending to do once I have accessed the deed, and damned if I don't, by instructing my solicitor to send a formal letter just makes me look like I am prepared to possibly enforce legal action against her living in the property, which is not the case – either way, it doesn't look good and sets the alarm bells ringing. My mother's reaction to all of this is to phone all of her friends in her phone book, and ask them have they heard the news about me, in what I have done, and more shockingly what I am intending to do, proves what she has known all along – that I am a bad egg. Probably not the response she was expecting to hear from the one person prepared to listen to her,

her one and only friend. If it were their daughter in this situation, they wouldn't be so quick to judge and give a harsh sentence. However, she takes no heed and is more than happy to accept the words of this man, whom she hardly knows, over her own daughter. Turning on the television and not dealing with this is my mother's way of dealing with it, in the hope that this will somehow disappear into space never to return.

To be able to continue with the abuse of psychological warfare, which the court cut short, Damian has had to find alternative ways to inflict the utmost emotional pain possible. What better way of doing this than using his key knowledge of my most painful experiences in my life, and forcing me to physically and emotionally relive them for the second time round, which has to be so intense, and more painful than you could ever imagine, that I am begging for his mercy, for him to end this. If not, I will wish I was dead.

Damian and his solicitor seem to think it is beneath them to be prepared for the fourth adjourned first FDR hearing. At a cost of one thousand five hundred pounds per hearing, it is not something they are going to lose sleep over, seeing how I am the one paying for it. Despite a two-month extension period granted by the court, the medical report requested by the judge has not been done due to their client waiting for a consultant to take him on as a patient. Based on this, his solicitor felt no need to instruct a further medical expert but asked if we would be agreeable to the consultant gastroenterologist performing the medical report, who has previously commented that the blackouts and other health issues appeared to be the result of the function of Damian's bowels. His solicitor lay the entire blame on the shoulders of my solicitor – had they acted sooner in querying them about the medical report, they would have quickly instructed another medical expert.

District judge three pointed out it that isn't the responsibility of my solicitor to ensure the work is done on Damian's file since he is not their client. With the lack of evidence being submitted there was no option but to adjourn the first FDR to be rescheduled for a further hearing. With court order stating a medical report must be submitted before the next hearing, along with confirmation of borrowing capacity, housing needs, costs, income, and assets, all evidence relating to any assets to be produced so all questions can be answered. It also stated that the dungeon was to be placed on the open market with an agreed estate agent. It is not my choice to sell the dungeon on the open market. I want to sell the dungeon by auction, and to have complete control of the sale. For this to happen I have to have good reason why this should happen, and evidence has to be submitted to the court. Apparently Damian's behaviour throughout the divorce, and FDR are treated as separate issues, so the court would require new evidence – evidence of him purposely delaying the sale of FMH (Former Matrimonial Home) provided by the estate agent, only then will auction be considered. This route has to be taken to give him the benefit of the doubt, just in case he has suddenly become a reformed decent human being. How many more times do we have to continually accommodate this man's behaviour? There is no doubt in my mind that he will delay the sale in any way he can. He is already being difficult by refusing the agreed estate agent to take internal photos, due to his sizeable private collector's items that are invaluable, this will encourage potential burglars to view the property in order to steal these very expensive items – the same expensive items that aren't worth anything, according to his Form E.

His collection is so vast it fills virtually the entire space inside, making it difficult to walk round the property. The estate agent would have suggested it to Damian, but seeing how the poor chap hasn't got the strength these days to possibly de-clutter the property, place these items into storage, fill in the cracks in the walls, which will need redecorating, and perform a thorough clean which would make the property more marketable, it is my responsibility to do so. He is clearly neglecting the property, and by doing so is devaluing it so my fifty percent becomes a lot less. When I tried to explain very briefly the difficulty of myself doing what they request, and the possible outcome if I attend the dungeon, the less than understanding estate agent's response was "well, someone has to do it." They want no involvement in any dispute between Damian and myself. I am not asking them to; their involvement is to sell the FMH as quickly as possible, and inform me of any problems arising in trying to sell the house, which will be dealt with through my solicitor.

My solicitor has gone on a sabbatical, and handed my case over to solicitor two in the law firm, who will now be my instructing solicitor throughout the case. They reassured me that, with two months before the next scheduled FDR hearing, solicitor two has more than enough time to be fully prepared and get up to speed with my case. A proposal for an out-of-court settlement was sent from Damian's solicitor, hoping by doing this that it will help me to resolve matters, bringing them to a swift conclusion, which their client is keen to do.

I must, however, bear in mind that when the house sells their client has nowhere to go. Their client hopes that I will accept how their current state of health affects them, and how difficult it has been for them to acknowledge they will never work again. He makes no money from the sales of his books, he has hardly sold any of them, and any money he does receive is donated to Christian Charities. I have to come to terms with his situation, and the difficulties he faces in finding a bungalow large enough to accommodate his requirements. Therefore their client requires ninety thousand pounds, with the remaining money from the sale to be paid to me in a lump sum. Each party is to pay their own legal costs, and a clean break in life and death. There are several points their client would like to draw to my attention – he has been more than accommodating in being actively involved in marketing the sale of the house, and a letter from the estate agent will confirm this. In relation to my allegations of harassment made against him, which have been investigated, their client maintains they are false, and has in their possession a letter from a chief inspector of the police confirming the harassment order made against him has been dismissed. In light of certain events, he feels he has been victimised in these proceedings, and that my lack of disclosure regarding the property that I own, combined with the allegations could amount to breech of conduct, which would be taken into account in terms of the financial settlement. By agreeing to this offer, they imply that I would avoid costs of future financial proceedings, which will be pursued if a settlement cannot be reached. Their client is making this proposal in an effort to bring a conclusion to matters.

By accepting this, I am in agreement to the proposed settlement and notification is required early enough so the courts are aware a resolution has been finalised. If however things remain the same, their client has already informed them, that he won't be able to attend the next hearing – with his mother being ill in hospital, he has no one to go with him to court.

I was a little taken aback by what I was introduced to upon my first meeting with solicitor two, who felt that a meeting with me two days before the FDR hearing was sufficient time to go through things. They launched into an almighty verbal attack against me. Did I realise how personally involved the previous solicitor got into my case? I was not to expect them to get that personally involved, because they won't. As far as they are concerned, I am taking the entire divorce proceedings all too personal by becoming too emotional. If I hadn't, things might have been resolved sooner. After reading the comments on Damian's proposed settlement offer, they demanded that it is about time I lay my cards on the table, and start telling them the truth, knowing the deed of trust was never fully in place and failing to disclose this will get me nowhere, except probably a lesser financial settlement as a result of my actions. There isn't a judge in the country that will grant me a fifty percent share of the FMH – I am not entitled to any of it. I cannot believe what I am hearing. Solicitor two, who is now representing me, is mentioning the possibility of having my mother evicted from what has been her home for the last twenty years, claiming she has no greater right to live there, since the deed of trust was never properly executed, and the house is jointly owned by all three of us, so in effect she could be made to move out if necessary. This way I can still afford to buy another property from the proceeds of the sale. Failing to do this, if Damian were to stake a claim on my third share I would end up in a worse position. How much worse can it get for me after the law firm you instruct keeps giving you the repeated sales pitch; "I can get you fifty percent, it is what you are entitled to," only to then say "No, you're not entitled to a penny from the property that you have paid into over the years." I have to pay the full mortgage every month to stop it from going into arrears, because the man who lives in it feels he doesn't have to pay it every month, just as and when he sees fit to. I also have to pay this law firm that I have instructed, who have backed me into a corner, in a hole so deep financially that I can't get out of it without the money from the sale of the FMH.

I have had to take out bank loans to pay their legal fees to get what was my fifty percent, which is now my fifty percent of nothing. They have put me in a position that I am unable to get out of. I have already paid twenty-three thousand pounds, and the future incurred costs that currently stand are so high that I am not in a position to instruct another law firm. To add to matters, they have provided me with this heartless solicitor two who is putting me in an unreasonable situation.

Their way of resolving this is by having to choose between evicting a woman that has lung disease, heart failure, and various other health issues from her home, so I can pay my debts off, or a bleak future I face of bankruptcy and homelessness. All this just so Damian can have what is rightfully his, a sizeable bungalow to home his vast private collections, to enable him to live the life he requires, so that he may continue writing more books whilst living off the state benefits, so he doesn't have to spend any of his savings made from monies earned from the sales of his books, or cash in his shares or pensions, to enable him to lead the life he needs, while he idles his time waiting to inherit the entire three hundred thousand pounds family home. It cannot get any worse this hell I am living in and what I am facing. It is wrong on so many levels to expect me to do this to my mother. I wish her well in her life, but she plays no part in my life or in these legal proceedings. I am certainly not going to pursue to have her evicted from her home, I couldn't do that.

Turning up late for the court hearing in a crumpled suit you could mistake for having been slept in, a shirt hanging half in, and half out of the waistband of the trousers – this was how solicitor two arrived. Outside of the court building, they had dropped all of the bulky documents that couldn't be contained inside the flimsy cardboard folder, the documents which they had been bringing to court. Trying to juggle these documents in the blustery wind with a take-away coffee proved to be a little more tricky than anticipated; which do you save, the coffee or the documents?

Whilst solicitor two frantically tried to save their coffee like a rabid dog, an immaculately dressed person so well-groomed with not a hair out of place, calmly walks past in shiny shoes, and appears to be commanding these falling documents to land in an effortless manner into their hands, which bizarrely they do, in a neat pile. They hand them over to dishevelled solicitor two, who has added coffee stains to their attire, whilst at the same time addressing their client, Damian, who has just arrived. District judge four, is sitting in

162

the hearing, on loan from another court to help reduce the impending backlog of hearings that the court are experiencing since illness has struck two of the district judges. Prior to the hearing district judge four had all but three chairs removed from the courtroom, and the table moved, to enable Damian's wheelchair to access the position where they wanted him to be – on the left-hand side of the square conference table, with his solicitor sitting next to him, and my position was on the right-hand side of the district judge, with my solicitor also sitting next to me. I was only informed of this enforced premeditated seating arrangement upon entering the courtroom by district judge four, who likes to look at both parties' faces during the hearing, as it gives a more informal slant to the hearing. Damian and I are directly facing opposite each other. This is not helpful – my throat is closing up and I can hardly breathe. I am biting hard on my bottom lip to prevent myself from crying; I know that, if I do, I won't stop, and I can't leave the courtroom with what is sitting waiting outside the courtroom in the narrow corridor – his parents. It just brings back the memory of being restrained by his father.

I can't do it, I just can't sit and face him for one hour and thirty minutes. The only way I get through this is by positioning the chair I am sat in, so the back of the chair faces Damian, to which district judge four remarked why didn't I turn my chair around so that they could see me? Solicitor two responded by saying that I am a little upset since the divorce, and that is why their client is not turning around. Not because I am fearful of this man who continues to abuse, and harass me in, and out of the courtroom, coughing my name or breathing as heavy as he would before starting the verbal attacks, to ensure I don't speak in the courtroom, and it works because I can't. At the moment I am not strong enough, and the one person I am relying on, at two hundred and fifty pounds per hour, will not do it for me. District judge four has already decided, within five minutes, from physical observation, including my entrance into the courtroom, my general appearance, and handling my Form E like they were shuffling a deck of cards, that my needs are currently in place because I have a job, therefore I have no needs in relation to the settlement of the divorce. Now is the time for solicitor two to say, well actually my client does have needs, and what those needs are, and why we are seeking this settlement, but instead they nod in agreement with district judge four's comments.

From this moment I am done, I have lost, I want no involvement with any of these hearings any more, or with this law firm that has wasted my time, money I don't have, and added to incredible amounts of stress I am under. I cannot show you my scars for they are hidden deep within me – they may not be evident to see, but I can assure you that they are there. I burst into tears for no apparent reason or at the slightest noise – it can be a gate being slammed shut, a car door closing, or, the worst for me, the sound of doors repeatedly opening and closing over and over again. Raised voices, people shouting to each other on the street, whether they are having a conversation or a heated argument, a man walking past me in the street, or standing next to me in queue in a shop or being on an over-crowded train, unable to move in confined spaces, and not being able to find my way out of a building, or speaking to anyone, and having a conversation – all of this puts me on edge. These constant triggers keep opening the wounds

I have, between the ongoing bouts of panic, and anxiety attacks throughout the day, where my heart is beating so fast it feels like it is going to explode out of my chest in fear, my clothes become soaked wet through with the excess perspiration, my throat tightens, and the whisper that comes is all there is. Frozen to the spot, my body becomes rigid in preparation for what is to come; my body has become so accustomed, it's like it is on automatic pilot. I not only have to live with these daily flashbacks, but I am forced to relive them again and again in the constant nightmares.

Whenever I walk outside I feel so unbalanced, the world is spinning around me so fast, it is making me dizzy. I can barely stand, all I want to do is crawl on my hands and knees on the floor, and go into a hole and never get out. I am so exhausted of fighting this losing battle with Damian, the courts and now solicitor two. How alone do I feel sitting in that courtroom? Even more ironic is the phobia I used to have has now become my ally – who would have thought a spider that came to sit with me would greatly help me whilst I am having to listen to Damian's solicitor defending their client?

They produce the letters from the chief inspector of the police and the estate agent; by providing this evidence, they set the scene, and adding the wheelchair convinces district judge four, who is so entranced by the great performance put on by Damian – he has district judge four wrapped around his little finger. The judge appears willing to do anything to help this sick man, including possibly enforcing the sale of my mother's home, even without the consent of my mother, my sister and I. We have to listen to an epic tale of how Damian has been in touch with my mother, whom he hates with a passion. During this emotional reunion, she informed her son-in-law of a proposed financial offer made to her by an entrepreneur property developer, who is wanting to develop the extensive garden by converting it into three houses. The offer my mother has received reflects the potential sale of these three new properties, in addition to the cost of purchasing her home in this package. This verbal information has secured my mother's home being taken into account in the proceedings.

If the offer being made is substantial, and is of greater value than of the market price of the FMH, then Damian is entitled to the entire FMH as the court sees it as unfair for one of you to have something more expensive than the other, so you have to have something equating to the same amount. If not, then the person with the lesser amount has to be given more, to tip the balance so you are both financially on an equal footing. A decision will be made on Damian's disabilities and care needs, and depending on the price of the sizeable bungalow required to cater for his future needs. If it is of a certain level he requires, then he will be entitled to a percentage of my third share of my mother's home, and if it is so great then he may be entitled to all of my third share. I cannot believe what I am hearing from these people, for how casual they are in what they are intending to do – Damian's needs have to be met regardless of others. They can quite easily justify these actions, and are readily prepared to make an ill woman homeless, without her consent.

Can they do this? How legal is all of this, a law firm with a solicitor that accesses a deed of trust even without consent of the person it refers to, and how ethical is it to continue to practice knowing full well, they have wrongly advised a client and, in doing so, they have placed them in a financial crisis, which they are aware of. Also, a district judge, as well as ignoring any monies earned from the sales of books, valuable collector's items, missing bank accounts, shares and pensions, decides that a woman with symptoms of post-traumatic stress disorder, brought on by the years of abuse from the man in the wheelchair, has no needs. Instead, forcibly selling someone else's home without their consent is in no way tipping the scales of justice to the man in the wheelchair pretending to be disabled. While all four of them in the courtroom are in agreement to when the next scheduled hearing will be, planning it like some old school reunion, I wish I could have made my escape like my ally, the spider, did, rather than having to endure the court order given by district judge four, requesting another medical report regarding Damian's health, prognosis, and what size property would accommodate his needs, which is to be submitted fourteen days before the next hearing.

Solicitor two seemed to think their response "a little upset" was appropriate, as was failing to mention the emotional and psychological abuse, being on the high-risk register, at risk of being murdered by this man, and having to wear a GPS unit. All of this is useless, in their opinion, to the hearing – I am being over emotional about all this. The court is only interested in dealing with the financial side – what you have and what he has. Anything else is irrelevant, unless he chopped my head off; then they would take gross misconduct into account. How worthless does solicitor two make me feel, their actions throughout this hearing speaks volumes.

Solicitor two is more than delighted that I have finally accepted, and come to terms with the situation, based on their advice they have given me. How deluded is this solicitor two? The proposed offer which I have asked them to send through to Damian's solicitor, offers him a sixty percent share of the FMH, plus the first nine thousand pounds from the sale, he keeps his pensions, and shares. It is not because I accept the situation – as hard as it is for me, I don't agree with any of this – but I feel I have been put in this position. I have no option if I want to stop my mother from being made homeless, for this man who is not ill, who continually harasses me by following me in the streets, sending implied threats of what may happen to me, all increased for added effect just before the court hearing to wear me down. All of this has me in such a state I have had to have hypnotherapy to try and help me speak, acupuncture to keep me calm and maintain my wellbeing, homeopathy to help with anxiety and counselling to get me through these hearings.

I have a solicitor who lacks any empathy, and has me tripping over Damian's wheelchair trying to rush me in the corridor down to the courtroom, fails to represent me in court in anyway, defending district judge four's actions in court with the seating arrangements insisting they were sympathetic to my position, and were fully aware of the abuse. With the estimated fees set at ten thousand pounds for the final hearing, there is no way I can get another loan to cover this cost. Solicitor two has informed me in the event that Damian refuses this offer, it will be listed for another hearing.

I have informed solicitor two that I will not be attending the hearing – there is no point of myself being there, as I have no needs in relation to the hearing. Apparently if I do this I run the risk of being arrested for failing to turn up to a court hearing, which won't look good for me in court. It is my entire responsibility to speak up in court, as they can't do it – what exactly does solicitor two do?

Whilst waiting for a response from Damian in relation to my offer, I have to find out if what he is claiming is true in relation to my mother's home, and has she signed any documents, unknowingly giving him an opportunity to access any proceeds resulting from the sale of the house she lives in. There is no other option – I have to contact my mother, and warn her of what Damian is trying to do. I feel sick dialling the telephone number, given to me by her only friend. When she answered, her voice was the same, and so was she – by denying life experiences, it resolves matters. How can you deny you had conceived, and given birth to a second child? This is what she did – she had no knowledge of who I am, or of ever knowing anyone of that name, and provided me with her only daughter's telephone number. Talking to sister is more than difficult. Like her mother, she cannot communicate and fears this, so she does it the only way she can – by constantly screaming at you or by resorting to violence. Mother's only daughter agreed to give me a few minutes of her time to hear what I have to say. I was to go to her mother's home to meet her there.

Inside my mother's home was the woman claiming not be my mother, my mother, sister, her husband and their daughter, along with her baby. I explained why I had to contact them, and asked if they had received any contact from Damian, or has anyone been out claiming to be a property developer offering an incredible deal. Mother, claiming not to be my mother, confirmed Damian has never phoned her. When I asked if he ever sent a letter, she accused me of calling her a liar and got out of her chair to leave the room in disgust at me turning up. Sister can hardly look at me, and when she does she can't hide the hatred she feels towards me. If it wasn't for the lies I tell, none of this would be happening; keep them out of it, it has nothing to do with them. She can see her words hurt me through the tears filling my eyes, and glories at her sick victory with a smile. Sister's wise husband, with his vast knowledge of the law (that you could fit on a pin head), did his calculations and, after counting to three, deduced the court can't do this. He sees it as three people against one; if anyone does come over here, he will beat them up. No matter how I try to explain, I can't get through to them, or how I am trying to stop this from happening – they need to be aware of what the court is prepared to do. Pretending this isn't happening isn't going to make it go away, and this vile disgusting person who my family think I am is having to accept a lesser deal from the FMH to stop the woman claiming not to be my mother from being evicted from her home. If my shoes was on my mother's or sister's feet what would they do? Quite easily they would be having me evicted without a doubt.

In the event that Damian does as he threatens, mother and sister will have to battle Damian together without me – I can do no more, I have my own battle to fight.

It is looking like the court hearing will be going ahead, after Damian's solicitor had contacted solicitor two in a letter indicating that there was further difficulties than they anticipated in relation to obtaining a medical report. This medical report the court has been repeatedly asking for, which never appears – why is no one questioning this? The gastroenterologist consultant, who Damian claimed to be under the care of, since the neurologist consultant had discharged him, cannot provide the medical report as Damian is no longer his patient, and having only met him once during a routine brief ten minute appointment, feels they are not in a position to. However, after being recently informed by their client, who is now undergoing treatment with a doctor who is a specialist in anaesthetics, and for pain management (medical acupuncture), they have asked this doctor to do the medical report for the court hearing. Failing this, they have in place a letter ready to submit to the court as medical evidence from Damian's practising GP, confirming their opinion regarding Damian's health. Due to the lack of improvement in the neurological symptoms, which greatly affect his mobility, it is difficult for him to return to any form of job in the future.

All of this is continually evading the truth – the fact that he is not as physically ill as he is leading us all to believe.

He has been pursuing the doctors in order to strengthen his case but he has finally exhausted all avenues, because they all have been presented with a difficult, aggressive man which none of them can treat. This means there is very little chance my case will get resolved, no district judge is prepared to make a decision without a diagnosis. With no one prepared to clarify what is non-negative terminal prognosis, this terrible affliction Damian has, apart from being an inherent liar, it means he can now live alone with little assistance from carers, but with seeing so many different doctors, and consultants at different hospitals he cannot remember which one of them gave him this diagnosis, in light of this new information it may bring clarity to resolving matters. A miracle has occurred, but it seems I'm the only one aware of this dramatic turn in events as the district judge doesn't tip the scale back in my favour in light of Damian's newfound health. Could it possibly have anything to do with the photographic, and video footage evidence I have of their client claiming to be so severely disabled that he is confined to a life in a wheelchair, and so incapacitated he is housebound?

How was he able to travel sixty miles, take a thirty minute walk up hill, knowing full well if he stands a few steps back from the lights at a very specific road crossing at an exact time of the day on a certain day of the week this will place him in a position so he is standing directly behind me, while I wait for the lights to change as I make my way back to work. If it wasn't for his distinct breathing that made the hairs on the back of my neck stand up, I wouldn't have known he was there. This was all done with clear intention to intimidate me as the court hearing draws nearer, by proving he can get away with what he is doing, and there is nothing no one can do about it. Feeding his own ego makes him a big man, strutting his stuff as he walks casually down the street, confident in what he is doing, acknowledging people in the street by smiling at them. So many witnesses but none who will help me, except for one he didn't count on.

For anyone who tries to help me, there are consequences – how can he make their life more difficult and what would hurt them? By doing this, no one will ever want to help me, therefore isolating me further. To relay his message, 'a taster of what is to come if you continue', what better effect than having the police turn up at your workplace to discuss your implied intentions of threats made against this sick man. He was minding his own business and happened to overhear a conversation between two people, one of them just so happens to be me – whilst he is waiting to cross the road, and what sounded like a direct threat made against his life, "that man needs stabbing," which brought back memories of his own attack of being stabbed in the back.

By manipulating the planned sequence of events, he can use it to his own advantage, by discrediting and falsifying people's actions into getting what he wants. He highlights how serious another person's behaviour is in order to distract the attention away from the truth of being exposed, and by doing so makes his behaviour look very minor in comparison. To have the involvement of the police – for any reported threat has to be investigated as a serious crime where there is intent to cause bodily damage – adds weight to his case.

Time is of the essence with the court hearing in a few days' time and he is aware he can no longer use the wheelchair as an act. He knows how to get the police's attention quickly, for he has them already jumping to his attention. Since they have failed to take seriously the attack that was made upon him, in an attempt to murder him, and as a result he lives in constant fear. He has taken it upon himself to provide further documentary evidence of the failings of the police officers at the time of the investigation. This has been drawn to the attention of the chief inspector of the police, whereby a full blown internal investigation into these allegations of breech of conduct, and of procedures that have failed to meet with the required legal standards governed by the laws in this country which he is well aware of, having spent many a time sitting in hearings, claiming to be an ex-county court judge. He makes it clear he won't be messed around by anyone – when he says jump, they ask how high your lordship?

They hoped once they had done what was expected, for there to be a full conclusion to end matters, except this ex-county court judge has never sat on the bench, only a park one. This was just a cover to get what he actually wanted. I was more than surprised to receive a direct phone call late one evening, from the chief inspector of police, to explain the event of circumstances which has evolved and as a result has forced them in contacting me. They have been trying to avoid doing so, as they are aware this is just another way of Damian maintaining the abusive behaviour. They didn't want to cause any undue stress but, in light of recent events, they strongly advise me to take out a non-molestation/injunction against Damian as soon as possible – they are concerned for my safety, and don't mean to scare me. Could I also help them with any information I might have relating to Damian's character? It may be a phone call, text message, letter, or past conversation where there might be discrepancies to the actual series of events – if there was anything I could think of, to call them on their direct line, as it would help further the investigations that have been ongoing for three months and has resulted in the chief inspector being placed in an unfortunate position. In order to stop the harassment they were personally receiving from Damian and to get him off their back, they waved the white flag to surrender to his demands, which was quite simply a signed letter from the chief inspector, dismissing the harassment order made against Damian.

Defending their action as appropriate, in their opinion I wasn't at that time in any great threat. What made me think I was? Did someone tell me I was, was that the case? I fail to see their reasoning, for someone in a position of authority who is supposed to have done a thorough investigation, claiming I never said the exact wording emotional or psychological abuse in any of the statements I have given to the police. Frightened, scared, and intimidated don't count. Had I used the correct words, then I wouldn't have placed this chief inspector in the impossible position and they could have done something, instead of letting Damian slip through the net, which they shouldn't have done. They had the option to do something, but instead they chose to sell me out because it is far easier to do so – the only difficult position is having to phone me at midnight to confess their failings, for now my safety is more at risk. They claim they are not in a position to do anything about this, their hands are tied, seeing how they have dismissed all allegations made against him. I have yet to meet anyone in a position of authority who is prepared to do the right thing and not give in to this emotional terrorist.

The list of reasons why solicitor two isn't submitting the photographic evidence two days before the hearing, claiming it is too late to submit this evidence to the court, and to his solicitor. It is not deemed relevant to the hearing, as he is not a murderer or attempted to murder me, and how sure can we really be certain that it is him walking? It's not going to help my case, I have to accept this.

Damian enters the court building to a sea of gasps, coming from the security guards as they stood with their mouths wide open in amazement at the astonishing recovery he has made as he walks past them, wearing the exact same clothes as in the photographic evidence. If this miracle recovery has the two security guards baffled, and questioning each other as to how it has happened, then why isn't solicitor two doing the same?

During the engagement of conversation between the two solicitors, the main topic into resolving matters at the hearing was that Damian needed to know why two people were sitting with me in the court waiting area. He wants them banned and evicted from the court building immediately. Under no circumstances am I allowed to have anyone sitting with me, is this understood? He pressurises his solicitor to implement his instructions, claiming to have been victimised, which is to be noted and recorded by the court, together with my actions throughout the legal proceedings. Failing to do so will result in him not going into the courtroom. It is all starting to fall apart, and crumble down on top of him. He is losing the plot, and this feeling of not having his tight control over me doesn't sit comfortably with him; trying to have me isolated is a lame attempt at regaining his control. As difficult as these hearings are for me, not once have I asked for his parents to be removed, despite the fact that they continually harass me, both in and out of court, by staring intently at me and mouthing speechless insults, and who have physically threatened me.

District judge five was sympathetic to my concerns when solicitor two relayed how distressing the hearings have been for me, and was happy to continue without me or Damian being in the courtroom. While each of our solicitors go into the courtroom to represent our cases to district judge five and, in relation to these matters, make their suggestions. The solicitors then leave the courtroom to inform both of us, who are sitting at the opposite ends of the court waiting area, what has been discussed in a bid to resolve matters. Both solicitors then have a further engagement of conversation. If nothing can be resolved, the solicitors go back into the courtroom, and discuss matters further with the district judge. This is repeated until an agreement has been made, or until you have run out of your allocated court time, or it is going nowhere, then it will be rescheduled to another hearing with court orders being made. Solicitor two heads in my direction to deliver the minutes of the first part of the hearing – Damian is now seeking a house with stairs and would also require a stair lift that needs to be fitted to enable him to access the upper level of the property. No actual medical report has been submitted, only the brief letter from his GP. District judge five feels there needs to be a medical report, and has suggested the consultant gastroenterologist perform this report, which should include any specific needs Damian has and what is Damian's future working capacity.

There is also to be taken into account his mortgage capacity and the sale of the FMH, which is to be placed on the open market. This district judge five has been drafted in to further help reduce the backlog of hearings, but they haven't fully grasped the full concept of the situation and are quite clueless even with all of the information placed in front of them. How many more times do the court have to request a medical report, and why is no one questioning why hasn't it been done? I fail to see what is the point in repeating this, when it is evident it is not going to get done. All Damian is doing is mirroring the district judge by claiming he is not in any position to be able to decide if my previous offer is acceptable, without having all of the medical evidence. What does need assessing is a report on Damian's mental health – this would give a clearer picture. In order for this to happen, he would have to consent to it as the court cannot enforce this. There is, however, a ten thousand pound difference based on the calculations, after taking into account my third share of my mother's home, and now my car has been added.

Previously it was excluded because, without it, I couldn't work – my job entirely revolves around me having the use of a car. According to district judge five's calculations, this has to be included. There is no value in the contents from the FMH to be taken into account, as his parents are claiming to have purchased every item from all the light bulbs to the custom-made three thousand pound settee these were gifts given to their son, and there is little value to be added from the one small rug I have bought.

If I were to offer Damian seventy percent, this would bring us on an equal footing – there would be sufficient money to fully purchase a property near his parents, and it just so happens solicitor two has the details of one property that has all the needs Damian is requiring. "Do it." With these words, solicitor two was gone in a flash to deliver my revised offer. They then return, throwing on the floor all of the pile of paperwork that they have had to carry in, and out, of the courtroom. They rant about how unreasonable that man is, admitting he has finally got under their skin – no one ever has managed to do that before. They have a good mind to report him to legal aid. For someone who doesn't do emotional or personal involvement, it was only a matter of time this would have happened, I can't say I am surprised, only welcome to the club, except their membership will shortly expire into a distant memory. Damian has refused the offer on the grounds the property is situated to the west, and it needs to be an east-facing property. If he were to be reported to the legal aid they would stop his public funding as all of his needs have been meet. The risk is, without legal representation he would have to represent himself which could result in this never being resolved. District judge five is probably hiding under the table and will not comment on the revised offer I have made, or intervene in helping with the situation. Today's hearing is well and truly over, possibly the fastest court order they have ever done, so they can make their quick escape.

Looking at the court order for the next scheduled hearing, my heart sinks reading when the medical report by the gastroenterologist and GP report is to be submitted to court, three different mortgage companies are to be approached on Damian's behalf, how much can he borrow to re-house being on benefits. Solicitor two goes to deliver my message – what will happen if Damian fails to accept? There is no other alternative with a district judge leaving the sinking ship and now solicitor two already feeling it's too risky and is more than ready to throw in the towel. His solicitor has given up as their client refuses to discuss the offer and will only talk about the affair he knows I am having with a woman. Solicitor two has demanded he put a stop to these allegations – they can't think of a worse insult than being called a lesbian. He has a ten day period in which to give an answer.

More mind games for the next ten days – he is going to put me through hell. This isn't the end of it all, he is gearing up for the next instalment, which he will use through the sale of the house to torture me further. Even if he does agree, he doesn't have to buy a property with the money; it is up to him what he chooses to do with the money, there is no legal obligation to do so. He could gamble it away or choose to live with his parents and spend the money. Solicitor two didn't think to inform me of this during the hearings, so what was the whole point of taking his needs into account?

The district judges revolved the whole hearings around him, and were prepared to make someone homeless, so the proceeds of their home can be used to purchase endless more DVDs, and more crap to fill his bedroom at his parents' home, and this is legal. I have no faith in this legal system that pretends to be something it is not.

He made sure I waited the full time before finally accepting the offer. The final detail is to confirm we are both in agreement to this by way of a consent order, a legally binding contract confirming Damian gets the first nine thousand pounds from the sale of the house. Then a further seventy percent of the proceeds of the sale, he will pay me a lump sum of ten thousand pounds for costs. We will both continue to pay the monthly mortgage payment, whereby Damian will pay seventy percent and I will pay thirty percent until the property is sold, and the joint bank account is to be closed with any monies equally divided. A clean break clause is added, meaning no further claims can be made against each other in life or death. By signing this, we agree to the terms we are bound to. Any breach in the contract will result in a court hearing, and further action being taken. Besides my few garden plants, all I am requesting are the photos of me as a child – there aren't many of them but I would like them back.

He is agreeable to my request but insists that I am not to enter the house – his friend will be there on guard inside to prevent me from going in and stealing from him. He has posted the photos to my mother's address.

An hour before I was due to collect my plants, a message had been delivered to solicitor two, requiring their urgent attention, regarding their client. If I do not collect the box he has placed outside next to the dustbins and remove it from the property, he will report me to the police for having possession of a dangerous weapon, which he has found inside the dungeon and carefully placed inside the box, knowing it belongs to me.

I couldn't believe the condition of the house when I arrived. The windows, which had to be constantly thoroughly cleaned so they gleamed, were smeared with mud, dustbins were piled in a heap on the ground at the front of the house, lying in amongst the mountain pile of rotting leaves. He used to forbid them ever to be located at the front of the house due to it being untidy – no house he lived in would look like a slum, so they had to be always kept out of sight in the back of the garden. There were also empty crushed drinks cans left outside lying on the front door mat. I walked down the driveway to the garden, past the long wooden fence –every panel was broken and tied with string, looped through each wooden panel in a bid to hold it together – I had to paint it twice a year to keeping it looking immaculate. The garden I had tended to was vastly overgrown and neglected, whilst my pot plants were either dead or dying, due to neglect or possibly being poisoned. The steps up to the balcony had been smashed, to prevent any access onto it.

A thick heavy-duty rusty chain had been fixed into the balcony wall, and pulled through the metal round ring that was attached directly across onto the wall of the house, secured with a padlock. This metal chain barrier had a sign hanging from it, emblazoned with a danger logo – hardly a warm welcome for any prospective buyer.

A cardboard box covered with various stains with the top of the box open – all of the sides had been folded inside and stapled to secure their position. To protect the open box, it was covered like a spider's web with layers of double-sided sticky tape, that covered the entire width, and length of the box. In between the gaps, the scrunched-up pieces of newspaper were pushing up, with it being so over packed, and not enough room with what lay beneath it all. Stuck underneath the layers of sticky tape was a visible note from him, scrawled in his left hand, to make it appear he hasn't got the ability to write clearly from having a stroke. Hoping I was well, and how he constantly worries about me, there are some letters that have been delivered here, and a few other items for me to take with me. To ensure I looked at all of the contents inside this box, he had to be certain I did, and claiming there was a dangerous weapon was a sure thing to get me to look. There was no dangerous weapon – just a sharps bin with used scalpel blades, and a weapon of emotional torment that he had been withholding from me for over eight years. Amongst the pile of advertisement letters, and opticians reminding me my eye test is well overdue, were other letters addressed to me that I wasn't aware of, some of which he had opened and kept hidden from me. A birthday card from my father with his new address and contact details; a photocopy of a letter from my mother sent shortly after the argument we had, saying how upset she was, and when was I going to visit her, for me not to take her dog as she couldn't cope without it.

There was also letter from a person claiming they didn't witness the road traffic accident involving the make, model, and car registration of the car that I owned, claiming they wanted no involvement in the fraudulent claim I have made to the insurance company. They confirmed they were never at the location of the accident which occurred on such day and time, and they are to be kept out of any legal prosecution – only the actions of the named driver living at this named address is to be prosecuted for using their identity and signature to seek car repairs through illegal purposes. What else has this man done to me that I don't know about? What did I ever do to him that he feels he can do this to me? He sees it fitting, and justified that he should implicate me in a criminal offence that I have had no knowledge of until now. How could he do this, all these years knowing how upset I had been over my mother, he kept asking me every time I went to collect the mail from the post box was there anything from her. For months he did this and, every time I went to collect the post, he had me checking through all the letters delivered individually in case I had missed it, or it had become accidentally stuck to another letter through being so tightly packed in the post person's mail bag. He had me doing this, all along knowing full well she had written to me, and he kept this hidden from me to prevent me from seeing her. It wasn't his choice to do so, it was mine, and he took that away from me. Who knows, maybe we would still be in contact, and talking to each other, I don't know. The only way I am going to know what is to come of my mother offering the olive branch is by contacting her.

For her to do this, and make an effort to resolve matters, isn't in her nature, so I feel I should at least try and meet her halfway to see if we can work things out. I thought the best option would be to write to her explaining what had happened, and why I hadn't received the letter that she sent all those years ago. This would give her time to process her own feelings, to decide whether she wants to talk to me or not. Two months later, my mother got in touch. We spoke on the phone – her life was still the same, glued to watching the television, watching the same programmes day in day out, and eating cake. Due to her ill health she can't do things, and has to rely heavily on her family to help her, as well as having the carers come twice a day to help her in and out of the bed, and getting showered. All the jobs I once did for her had all been distributed throughout the family – her daughter takes her to the doctors, and hospital appointments. She feels bad for putting on her, as it must get her down having to constantly do this. Whilst her grandson collects her pension, pays the bills, and takes her to the local supermarket to get her weekly groceries. Her granddaughter comes to clean the house, changes her bed does her laundry, and keeps her company with her baby. She doesn't reckon much to her other granddaughter, who she rarely sees and thinks is odd because she has a medical condition. She can't remember what it is but it makes her cry a lot – an odd girl, she won't do anything for her. She knows how difficult divorce is, what with hers, and tells me all about this.

She forgets I was the one that helped her through it all – filling in the paperwork, attending court hearings, supporting her emotionally and financially. It was like she had completely erased me from all aspects of her life. All she repeatedly asks me is have I got a fella yet; I say no and try talking to her about the symptoms of post-traumatic stress disorder I have, which brings an abrupt end to the conversation (with an excuse like 'not realising the time of the day, her arm needs to rest as it is aching from holding the phone'). The conversation at the next phone call wasn't what I was expecting to hear from my mother, who has very limited vocabulary. I heard her say the words I haven't heard for a while, the exact words, words she doesn't use, words that only came from Damian's mouth. She repeated them back to me exactly in the same context as he did, always at the start of his verbal interrogation; "Can I ask you a question, can you explain to me why?" This triggered a response inside me. Immediately, the automatic walls inside me shot up so quickly around me, I could feel myself sinking into the ground as these walls grew taller and taller, so tall I couldn't see above them, to get out. I need to get far away from her as quickly as possible. She waits in silence at the end of the phone for a response from me which I can't give, to why I didn't go to her when I left him. My throat is closing up, I go back to losing my voice, all I can do is cry, and put the phone down to make my escape. How would she know these words unless she spent time with him? I don't know if I can do this, and have some sort of relationship with her.

Could she have coped with what state I was in after I had made my escape? She couldn't cope having me as a child, so how she would have dealt with the aftermath if it presented itself on her doorstep? In times of trouble or difficulty she had always turned to her youngest child, who became her mother, to sort it out; for twenty-three years I was forced into being a parent to her. This made me very self-reliant – the Wendy house I took to the fields was my home, I had already moved out in my mind and was earning money from selling sweets. If I ever went to ask my mother for anything she would shout at me to shut up and go away. For me to go and ask her for help was never an option for me, probably because I knew what the answer would be. These routine phone calls where I listen to my mother tell me all her troubles, and about her family life is all that she has. She avoids anything relating to the past or my present life as she has no interest or desire to know. When I test the water with information I feel I want to share with her, what book I have read, she doesn't know how to interact with me. The child she had isn't doing what it used to do; instead, it is no longer trying to constantly please her or avoid upsetting her by her feel inadequate about something I have done and she hasn't. She cannot handle being expected to reply back to this second child, this is not what she is used to. She doesn't know what to do and resorts back to silence, like she would do when I was a child. I would feel I had done something bad when she did this and in order to get her to speak to me, I would plead for days on end for her to say something to me, begging for her forgiveness so that she may love me again.

Her terms and conditions aren't working like they used to. I suggested I thought it might be a good idea if we meet, to talk about what has happened, as I thought it might help us try and resolve things, and move forward to form some form of relationship, rather than having these meaningless conversations, which I could have at the supermarket or in the street. However, it brought the call to a swift end as she had just seen the time; it was lunchtime, at ten a.m. There was a message on my voicemail the day after from her saying she didn't want me to go and visit her, she didn't want to see me, or talk to me ever again, it would be too painful for her to talk about the past, she hasn't got the time as she is too busy with her family. No matter how long I sit on the pavement waiting for the bus to come and stop, and open the doors with my mother's love, it is never going to come. The relief from my mother's actions gave me peace, and freed me to get up from the pavement and cross the road, because I don't have to wait any more.

Enter the wooden horse

Estate agents either wear rose-tinted sunglasses or are very good at lying. This skilled valuation process of your house which requires detailed information from all of the relevant properties that have sold within your area over a period of x amount of years, and in conjunction with all this, the condition of your house all has to be taken into account – this all calculates to zero. Basically it all boils down to you, to name your price what you want to market it at, they in turn will tell you they can get you this. There is nothing that these people can't do, walk on water, swallow rods of fire. Any problems or concerns that you might have, they can resolve in an instance, in a desperate attempt to prevent you from going elsewhere by feeding you these delicious sweets so you won't go elsewhere, why would you, when they are giving you everything you wanted. In return they get the commission fee they charge from the sale of your property, which you agree to by signing a contract to all their terms and conditions. Their glossy information package, complete with testimonials from previous sellers and buyers relaying their experiences, plus why they feel you have made the right choice in choosing them to market your property, fills you with hope and certainty that you know they are going to do the utmost to sell your property. Maybe they should have added in small print that, if you do not live at the property, they will not inform you of any booked viewings or give you any feedback on any viewings because it is not their job – it is the responsibility of the seller to contact them every week. They keep no records whatsoever about the viewings, and rely heavily on storing this information in a filing system in their minds.

Their alternative approach in selling your property is by a unique technique called let's wait and see what happens, whereby if someone happens to enquire about your property only then will they offer a brochure. At a push, in between the endless mugs of coffee, cigarette breaks and the office competition as to who has the best manicured nails, they might try and book them in for a viewing. Failing that, if no one asks about your property, they can't be held responsible for it not selling as it is not their job, or the manager of the estate agent. Someone has to get involved and be proactive in marketing the dungeon, if not it will never get sold. Two viewings in four months and no further bookings. I had no option but to contact solicitor two who is of the same ilk as the staff members at the estate agent – it is not their job to get involved. As far as they are concerned, it is an estate agent issue, not one that requires their legal services, because Damian has been compliant with all the viewings, he hasn't refused anyone going so there isn't really an issue. It could simply be down to a lull in the market, or that it will be one of those long-standing properties that take time, possibly months or years to sell. I can't wait years for it to sell. I am tired, tired of hanging off the edge of the cliff with my bare fingers clinging on for dear life, not being able to let go and fall into pieces after hitting the ground below me, having to be the constant driving force behind it all so I can reach my goal, which is to have an end to all of this, so I can fall in order to heal from the trauma Damian put me through.

It was only when Damian's solicitor contacted solicitor two about the conduct of the estate agent which raised concerns to their client about their capability in marketing the property, and asked if I be in agreement in changing to another estate agent, this is when solicitor two took notice of the situation. Between all three of them I was delegated to find another estate agent, which then had to be approved by Damian, who agreed to estate agent two. They were very understanding about the situation with it being less than amicable, and the only form of communication we have between each other is through the solicitors. They reassured me this wasn't a problem – they would discuss separately with us about booked viewings and feedback. Within a couple of weeks there were a few booked viewings, the feedback was that it needs a lot of work doing, needs knocking down, and rebuilding. Steadily over the months an influx of booked viewings, with over thirty viewings, all of them with the same repeated feedback but no offers were being made. Each time I cross my fingers, and desperately hope this is the one – I am almost willing each and every one of them that goes to view the dungeon to buy it – only to have my hopes blown away. Until one day, when an offer was placed. Due to the condition of the dungeon, and the amount of work it would take to do the repairs, the person wanting to buy the dungeon felt it was an appropriate offer at thirty thousand pounds below the asking price. The consent order that we both signed is very specific; it clearly states at what price the dungeon is to be sold.

Would I be held accountable for breaching the consent order if I did accept this offer? It doesn't come with a manual explaining all the possible eventualities that may arise, and as a result what you can and can't do. Depending how you look at the consent order it is open to interpretation, so solicitor two informs me. If we are both agreeable to this offer then there isn't an issue. However, if I wanted to accept and Damian doesn't, to ensure he isn't at a financial loss as a result of the sale, I would have to pay Damian the difference – a further seventy percent of the thirty thousand pounds from my share. They suggest this is something for me to consider, as it would resolve the problem with the mortgage payments. Although he has breached the consent order by continuing to fail to pay, or is so late paying that it is three weeks overdue, this is justified by solicitor two's interpretation that technically he has paid, even though he hasn't, because he pays it in another month, but it is not every month, which it clearly states in the consent order. What is clear is solicitor two's interpretation is for Damian's benefit. With what they are suggesting after calculating the difference, it would leave me still in debt and unable to pay my loans off. A rather shocked solicitor two can't quite believe how little money I am getting. I am not in a position to be able to purchase another property, so my only option is to rent for the foreseeable future. They deny that they knew anything of this when they represented me. It is not acceptable, they are covering their back from being sued.

So the torture continues every day, hoping today will be the day when the estate agent phones to say another viewing has been booked – but nothing. All avenues had been exhausted – all of the property developers have been contacted,

191

advertisements in the newspaper, email brochures have been sent listing it as a property which is an ideal home for a first-time buyer or to invest in – it had come to a complete stand still. What happens now? Clearly the price is an issue – with the most number of viewings a property has ever had at their branch, and only one offer has been made. Estate agent two thinks it is a little strange more offers haven't been made – it is in a great location, with potential to make a profit. They are confident that the right price will attract a buyer in light of the statistics they keep informing me of – sixty online hits viewing the dungeon, that is a fifteen percent increase from last week. I find it is totally useless, they are just number crunching. I don't care about that, it is not getting results. In their defence, fifty viewings resulted in not one but two offers being made, both of which were declined. Basically, you are at fault for not accepting. How could I accept the second offer if I wasn't informed of it in the first place? Nor was I informed of the viewing that took place some weeks ago, which resulted in the offer being made, only to be rejected by Damian simply because it was eight thousand pounds less than what he wanted. I was not given the opportunity to accept this offer, merely informed about it because my name is the second one to be written on the file, meaning it is not classed as the lead name. The first one written down on the file is the main source of contact, and with him residing in the house he has overriding preference.

I feel this offer is more than reasonable given the comments from the past viewings, and unbelievably so does solicitor two who suggests that we need to know what the estate agent two thinks to this offer – whether they think the same and, if they do, would they confirm this in writing as it would enable us to force the sale through at this price. The difficulty would be waiting for a court date for the hearing, during which time you may lose the buyers, and more so if they know it is due to a divorce settlement. Estate agent two had no comments about the offer, other than they were confident in achieving the full asking price. Regardless of the previous comments about how much work it needed doing, they expected to do this within three months. The slight mix-up should have never happened, every effort has been made to prevent a recurrence. Estate agent two informs me of the action taken – number one, all staff have been informed, and number two, using a marker pen written in big letters emblazoned across the file, 'contact the second-named seller of all viewings and offers'.

The high expectations of the sales staff at estate agent two didn't meet the targets they had set themselves, including reading the file to inform me of the ten booked viewings, and selling the dungeon at the full market price. With no offers coming they suggested it needed to be marketed for a lower price and suggested a three thousand pound reduction to generate interest. This price suited Damian but he wasn't prepared to accept any lower offers, with the further reduction.

With estate agent two's confidence there is no limit in what they can achieve. By confirming this with Damian, he will hold them to this verbal agreement – if they fail or try to back out, it can only result in war, which he intends to win. The chances of this happening are very limited. Unless you have an absolutely fantastic house, you will not get the price you want; if it is a bit of a dump that needs a bit of work doing, you are not going to get a fantastic price. To pre-empt losing out on a future sale, I asked estate agent two could they confirm in writing what would be a reasonable minimum, and maximum price for the dungeon to be sold at. Apparently they can't discuss this with me, only with a solicitor who would have to write to them directly to request this information. Bureaucracy gone mad! Solicitor two was somewhat disgruntled; they should not be having to directly contact them. Do they not know the rules of engagement? Clearly not, or they don't care. I wished they did as I would not be having to pay solicitor two to send a letter to them requesting this information, who will then, at a further cost, send me a copy of the letter they have received from estate agent two. What is this all about? To see who can bark the loudest?

After a review of six months of marketing with the new price, there had been no more booked viewings so estate agent two decided the only was way to make an impact. It would have to be greatly reduced by five thousand pounds – they would put this to Damian to see if he was agreeable.

This would take it down to the value of the second offer, when, at the time, estate agent two had commented that they were capable of getting the full asking price. Now they wanted to market it at the price that had actually been offered. They have lost a potential sale. This could have been all done nine months ago, I am so upset that this could have been resolved sooner. The day after, I received a letter from estate agent two saying they have been put in a difficult situation and can no longer market the property, suggesting we get another estate agent to market the dungeon. There was no mention when they were pulling the plug on the dungeon – was it immediately or in a few days' time?

An abrupt member of staff at estate agent two – who shouldn't be talking to me, but felt the need to release their feelings to me, and in no uncertain terms – lay the entire blame at my door, claiming if I had been more reasonable and talked to Damian, none of the staff would have been placed in the difficult position they have been put in. By confirming this in a letter, as far as solicitor two was concerned, it showed me in a bad light. They wouldn't want the court to see this – heaven forbid – because my intentions of wanting to sell a house is far way worse than the lies and deception Damian has continually undertaken throughout the legal proceedings. To be fair, it is as long as it is broad – he doesn't want to sell I do. His implied threats to sue, and his aggression, also mixed with estate agents two's error in having to admit that the dungeon needs to be reduced to a price that was previously offered, which they had refused, claiming it was too low, meant that discarding us is their only option to save themselves.

Solicitor two knew all along about the difficulties in selling and why the estate agents don't want to get involved – it isn't an easy routine sale. If they already know this, then why isn't it going to auction to be sold, rather than being kept on the open market? It is still the same end result, which is to get it sold. This continual need for evidence – no matter how much I give them, solicitor two finds every other way from acting upon it – and not being prepared is their greatest downfall into failing to resolve the situation.

So my torment goes on. With no one marketing the dungeon, it is nowhere nearer to getting sold, and for it to go back on the open market depends on which estate agent Damian would be agreeable to. I have to get three quotes from three different estate agents so solicitor two can send these to him for his approval. How long will this take? It could be weeks before he decides, and to whether or not he has received this in the post is another issue to add to the delay. I am more than shocked when one of the estate agents who I just happened to go in to, informed me they were already marketing the property with the dungeon's address as the owner had already instructed them. The internal and external photos had already been taken, and were ready to go to print for the sales brochure to go on display inside the estate agents. The estate agent valuer knows all about the situation, so why wasn't I informed?

After a lengthy discussion with Damian, they both agreed to a price the dungeon should be marketed at, which just so happens to be the original price the dungeon was first marketed at eighteen months ago. This arrogant property valuer is Damian's new best friend forever. They claim they can get the full asking price and know all about the previous estate agents, pointing out their failings – it was marketed all wrong by making out it is something it is not. Raising the price is a clear indication that it is a greater property than what it actually is and this is somehow going to sell it. Based on this, there is no way I can get a price reduction on the dungeon, due to this estate agent's opinion. Solicitor two informs me that I have to go through the whole process again of having viewings and depending on the feedback, and to rely on what the estate agent suggests to sell it. It would be wise to let them market the dungeon seeing how Damian has been active enough to sort it out. I have no option but to have estate agent three market the dungeon.

When I suggest to solicitor two that I would like to have an estate agent of my own choice to also market the dungeon, this is out of the question due to the complications. If the house is sold, there would be a dispute over which estate agent sold it, but not if they were at a different price. Also they have their own separate records of who they have booked for the viewings, I fail to see why this obstacle has to be placed here, probably for Damian's convenience so he isn't inundated with viewings.

This unique estate agent three is happy if you are proactive in trying to sell your home by making it welcoming, and appealing, but, if you are not in a rush, just kick back and relax; they will give you all the time in the world trying to find you a buyer for your eventual move.

During the first three months of marketing the dungeon, estate agent three had contacted one hundred and three developers and potential buyers, but no offers had been placed and the feedback from the viewings was less than positive, with one saying they wouldn't have this house even if someone paid them to buy it – they wouldn't let a dog live in it; it needs bulldozing and rebuilding. Estate agent three suggested the price needs lowering, and Damian being Damian reminded his best friend forever that they had broken their promise to him by suggesting this, and also for talking to me about it, and, worse still, for confirming their opinion which was that it wasn't going to sell at the price it is marketed for. Because of this, Damian felt the need to threaten someone very close to me, my love, by sending through the post in an envelope twenty-five loose razor blades.

His intent is very clear: to cause physical damage, with positioning two blades placed in the crease of the fold where you seal the envelope, so when you come to open the envelope with your fingers it would cut them – his sole purpose is to harm this person, who has done nothing wrong. In his eyes, however, they have, by loving me and supporting me.

Knowing full well the police wouldn't do anything because he had worn gloves, there was no note inside or anything to connect him to this, other than he is the only person that would stencil each letter written on the envelope. They had nothing on him. Although they suspect it is Damian, if they contact him it might make him worse, so the advice of the police officer was to do nothing and put it down to a hardware store sending them through the post. How can you when you know this isn't the case? If it were, I wouldn't be contacting the police. Doing nothing doesn't makes his behaviour any better; it just allows him to continue to intimidate and threaten. At what point will the police intervene? When it is too late, and he has actually cut, tortured and possibly stabbed someone to death because they failed to take action when they could have, given his previous actions for the last five years. If this emotional terrorist becomes a bigger threat to national security, only then will they take notice. Solicitor two isn't interested – they just tell me that they have made an application to the court in relation to the dungeon – this is to get it reduced after all the contacts and viewings. It is clear it needs reducing – they will be in touch nearer the time.

After five more booked viewings, I find it more than strange. All the viewings were done separately, and at different times of the day, but each one of them gave the identical feedback as each other. What are the chances of all of them repeating the same context, word for word?

How did they all come to the same decision – the electrics are in a state, kitchen walls need knocking down, and all the floorboards need ripping up and replacing – when not one of the viewings took a builder with them? So how did they all deduce these very specific areas of work needed to be done to make it habitable? All of this raises more questions that point in the direction of Damian's deliberate act of sabotage in selling the dungeon. Estate agent three is oblivious to any underhanded tactics – no such thing would ever occur because nothing like this has ever happened in their world of property sales – probably because no one ever like Damian has ever entered it. With their head in the clouds, blocking their vision, they can't see anything wrong – it is just that their personal comments all happen to be the same. I do not accept this flippant excuse. I have no idea what is going on, or what is being discussed during the viewings, but the picture that is forming is not looking good with estate agent three, who is not prepared to get involved.

I have no option but to find someone who will be my eyes and ears for twenty minutes, someone neutral who is not connected in any way to either myself or Damian – that someone is a private investigator posing as a potential eager buyer. They made initial contact with estate agent three, who immediately informed the private investigator that the seller was difficult and can be hard to get hold of – already setting the scene even before you have stepped into the dungeon – it is going to be a hassle and very difficult.

They waited two weeks for a date to be confirmed, and a further week to finally go and view the dungeon. The private investigator has been informed by estate agent three that Damian will be showing them around the dungeon. I prepped them with the questions I wanted them to ask during the viewing, to see what Damian's response would be to them and whether he would try to put them off. This was the only way to know for sure what was happening behind the closed doors of the dungeon. The private investigator was not greeted by Damian, but by his mother as her son is too severely ill to show anyone around. The guided tour went into each of the dark rooms, with the curtains all closed and no lights switched on, and the private investigator had to be navigated around the piles of boxes so as not to walk into them. None of the rooms were clean, the general state of the dungeon was that it was being neglected, and needed updating inside and out, with the garden overgrown.

This, combined with Damian's father's personality being less than approachable as he gave his sales pitch about the price being non-negotiable, claiming it has already been reduced, is hardly being shown in a positive light to encourage any potential buyer. I was more than shocked to hear one of the previous viewers had actually placed an offer on the dungeon, and more shocked, given the condition of the dungeon and what this private investigator had gone through, that they had not put these buyers off, who had offered the full asking price. They had been twice to view the dungeon and were so eager to buy it.

Damian flatly refuses to acknowledge confirmation of this offer that has been made, by choosing to ignore all of the voicemails, and emails that estate agent three has been leaving since the offer was made five days ago. If this continues, the sale will be lost. Estate agent three will not move forward until they have both parties' agreement and, until this point is reached, they can do no more.

They are going to let it fall through even though the full asking price has been achieved. We have both signed a terms and conditions form agreeing for them to market the property at the price agreed, which has now been offered. They have received a letter from solicitor two explaining the legality of this. Whether or not he accepts, the optimum price, which is the full asking price, has been achieved and legally this can go through. Even after receiving this letter, they still dither about should they or shouldn't they confirm the offer, when they have all the relevant information and documents in front of them confirming it all to go ahead. The only reason that is stopping them is fear of this man and what he will do. They have already experienced his temper before and, by making them afraid by whatever means (probably with the threat of suing), he ensures that they toe the line. To stop the noose around their neck from getting any tighter, they gave themselves a little more time with one last desperate attempt to contact Damian – this would be the decider. Finally, they agreed, without Damian's acceptance, to exchange conveyancing details, and to inform the buyers their offer has been accepted.

Damian's only response was to send a deepest sympathy card. Written on the envelope, stencilled with the ink of a felt tip pen, was my home address which the bank had provided him with. Using rubber gloves so as not to get my fingerprints on it, I carefully opened the envelope, exposing a Stanley knife blade with the tip pointing upwards – it had been placed securely to ensure it would cause physical damage to my fingers or hands. Inside there was another blade, and a stencilled message written in the card. To make sure I know it is him that has sent this death threat, there is one letter that he hasn't stencilled, he has written in his own handwriting. He stood behind me, or my love, in the street, he overheard us talking, and we would not be waking up, we would be fucking dead. It's clear in his message that the two blades are meant for me and my love – who he had previously sent the twenty-five blades to – and what his intentions are. Surely the police will have to take this more seriously?

The police had a warrant out for Damian's arrest to take his fingerprints as he wasn't responding to them to go in for questioning about this. His parents could not help them locate their son, as they are unaware of his current whereabouts, but they would be sure to pass the message on if he contacts them. One week later housebound disabled Damian arrived at the police station with his solicitor in tow, to answer any questions. He denied any involvement in sending the death threat. The card and the blades went to forensics to be tested for Damian's fingerprints – if there were traces of his fingerprints, it may result in him receiving a cautionary warning for threatening behaviour.

It took fourteen weeks for the results to come back but no traces of Damian's fingerprints were to be found. There were marks on the card indicating gloves had been worn, and the letter he had written on the card didn't match his handwriting. With the investigating police officer having been taken off the case due to a complaint Damian had made about him, it has been put forth to the CPS (Crown Prosecution Service) to get involved as they have the time and resources to delve more into investigating cases. After reviewing my case, and taking into account the reported harassment, and PPU involvement, they don't want to get involved seeing how I am privately funding my own legal matrimonial case, and they suggested I fund my own legal prosecution against him. Just because nothing was found doesn't mean he won't slip up the next time is the police officer's theory to this problem I have, and the only way to resolve it is to keep reporting these incidents. This is somehow supposed to reassure me, when they do nothing other than allowing this man to continually abuse me.

What advice are they giving Damian? Is he being monitored, what changes has he had to make to his life? None. He can come and go as freely as he wants to, while I am the one who has to continually move away from him and adapt to prevent his behaviour interfering in my life, because it is easier for the police, the law courts and the entire legal system not to get involved.

By ignoring this man, it fuels his fire and makes him feel more powerful in what he is openly doing which just encourages him more. As the arrogance grows inside him, the more he craves power, and they give it to him by allowing him to do this to me. This deeply concerns me – he clearly feels threatened with the house sale and this is his reaction. He is losing his grasp of being in control over me – when the dungeon is gone, there is nothing left for him. This man that I pity is making sure he puts every obstacle he can in my way to prevent this from happening. There is no level he is not prepared to go to in order to keep being in total control – I believe he will do whatever it takes, including physically hurting anyone who helps me or who is in my life and stands in his way of being in control.

His desperate attempts are intended to keep me inside, away from the outside world, so I wouldn't go to the office of the conveyancing solicitor to enable them to start working on the dungeon being sold, with an estimated completion date in eight weeks' time when the keys would be handed over to the buyers. There is no way I am going to lose this sale, I have waited so long for it, and here it is. The pressure for Damian is mounting, especially when he received papers bearing my signature the day after the offer was agreed, confirming that they are to be the instructing conveyancing solicitors, which requires his signature confirming that he agrees to this. This is a legal requirement regardless that we had both agreed to on the consent order, and both signed instructing this firm – whom Damian demanded – to do the conveyancing work for the sale of the dungeon.

It still has to be signed so they can proceed with the work that needs to be done. He claimed to have never received any such forms, even though four lots had been sent through the post, and when he finally did receive them, he requested a further one to be sent, a fresh one without my signature on – he had to be the first one to sign any papers. It took him two weeks to sign and return the forms back to the conveyancers, and, as a result, I had to go back to their office and repeat by signing the forms again. Upon my visit I was asked to take a seat, the conveyancing solicitor would like to see me. They showed me the fixtures and fittings forms, and the buyers information pack – it basically lists what is being left in the property you are selling – light fittings, appliances in the kitchen, the cooker, fridge, what type of windows are there, has it got central heating – all relevant information with spaces available for further information that the seller can write and comment in. Damian did his best to do so in his scrawled handwriting – he is disabled and needs time for moving with his disabilities; he needs my keys delivered to him, and I am the one who is responsible for cleaning the property.

He knows full well that these forms are sent to the buyer so they can see what they are buying. This is more than enough to put anyone off, and the immediate question that comes to mind is how much time does he need? He is wanting is to put them off, and this would have the desired effect, not just with the buyers but also with the conveyancing solicitor who has never come across a person like Damian. He has intimidated them to the point that, just after one week of dealing with our case, they were considering whether or not to sack us – they personally felt threatened by this man's actions. It was such a relief to hear someone actually be honest enough to admit this. Not even the estate agents, police or the chief inspector have had the guts or been strong enough to not let his actions stop them from doing their job, but this conveyancer, isn't prepared to play games with him and is sticking to the task in hand, which is to do the conveyancing on the dungeon. Without them, the sale would have probably already been lost before it had a chance to get going. Imagine having to inform the buyers that I am waiting for a date for a court hearing, in order to get Damian to agree to another conveyancer acting on the sale of the dungeon, and this could delay the sale by a further six weeks. All the relevant paperwork at this stage of the sale has been completed by Damian – there is still more to be signed and to be agreed, but, at this point, no more can be done other than waiting for the buyers to get back to us with any queries they may have in relation to the fixture forms and buyer information pack.

There is a month to go before the court hearing, which was initially requested to apply for application so that the dungeon can be reduced in order for it to sell, but, seeing how there is an offer in place and no more papers can be signed at this stage, is there any need to go to court at this point? Everything has changed from what we were initially applying to do.

Solicitor two is adamant the sale is more than likely going to be lost, not just through Damian's actions, but also in case the buyers get made redundant, and wouldn't be in a position to continue to buy it. This is why the application to court has to go ahead, in case it needs to be re-marketed, and it can't be postponed at this late stage. It has to go ahead with the original proposal – it cannot be changed, it's going ahead whether I like it or not. Given the circumstances, I felt there needed to be an action plan to try to eliminate any future problems that may arise during the sale, in which Damian will no doubt delay matters further. "Let's wait and see what happens," is all solicitor two can suggest. This isn't the time to take a back seat and be flippant – this makes no sense in resolving my case. I fail to understand the logic in this, especially with all the past evidence there is to come to this decision. I received an almighty backlash from solicitor two, who claimed that what I was asking is illegal (to act on something that hasn't happened), not to mention the consequences. They need to remind me that this would place them in a difficult position that could lead to them being struck off, and myself being prosecuted and possibly imprisoned as a result. As I fail to respond to their outburst regarding my questions, which they have completely taken out of context (simply having an action plan and being prepared is all I am asking them to do), they have resorted not only to sulking with me for failing to engage further with them (by repeatedly reminding me of this in further correspondence), but also by what you would call sly underhanded tactics; if I don't pay my bill immediately, they can't proceed with the work they need to do.

The twenty-eight days in which they allocate you in their remittance statement to pay appears to have gone out of the window, so has their notification of their new payment scheme – they have failed to notify me of the changes that have all of a sudden been introduced, possibly just for me alone. In four years I have paid them forty-two thousand pounds and not once have I missed a payment or paid late. I have done all that they have asked – I am not a lawyer and I have no legal experience, so I will have questions and need a solicitor who is able to answer them and be professional enough to work with me, rather than against me in continually trying to cite an argument. I don't need to be battling with my solicitor and I should not have to be continually giving them at court hearings a typed action plan to attempt to resolve matters, which has been prepared by my love to fight my case. I am exhausted to the point I cannot do this anymore. I need a solicitor who is prepared to fight this battle for me, which solicitor two isn't prepared to do. Their "suck it and see what happens" approach is remaining silent in response to the letter I received from another solicitor, claiming to be acting on behalf of their client Damian. They warn against me continuing to report him to the police with these false allegations – they are referring to their client being questioned over the death threat which contained Stanley knife blades. If I continue to harass their client, who is severely ill and disabled, they will take further legal action against me. I felt I had no other option than to seek further legal advice from another solicitor, before going I wrote down briefly about where I was at with the hearings.

Also I wanted to know what they would do in trying to resolve my situation. Immediately this solicitor told me of the complications I would face, without knowing the entire details of the past four years – you have to have an action plan to block his routes, so his options are limited. This guru solicitor not only gave me valuable advice about having contact with the buyers throughout the sale, but also suggested ways to make it easier being in the courtroom. If I found it too traumatic, I didn't have to go as long as I could be contacted via a phone – I could be sitting in a café while the hearing was happening, I had a choice, but more importantly they were sympathetic, and understanding and they didn't make me feel worthless. Finally there was hope in sight – they could take over my case after the hearing if I decided I wanted them to represent me.

I sat waiting for solicitor two to turn up for the court hearing, unaware they were already in the court waiting area, for you cannot see around the corner where they were sitting. For me to do this, I would have had to walk past Damian, and his glaring posse whose looks could kill me given the chance. Solicitor two cannot comprehend how uncomfortable this may be for me, or what possible consequences could arise from me doing this. Not only was solicitor two disgruntled they had to be the one making the effort to find me, they had also been physically given, with only minutes to go before the hearing, a thick-paged detailed dossier all typed up and produced by Damian who was representing himself in court.

The severely ill Damian, who cannot work due to his severe disabilities, has managed to produce another lengthy detailed dossier, with evidence he has entirely gathered himself – letters from various estate agents, all confirming, after their valuation, that the dungeon should be marketed for a higher price and confirming that it was a delight to have finally met with him, showing him in a good light. It also included evidence of my behaviour – exhibit marked Damian four – the letter he had sent to me about harassing him, and reporting him to the police. He went on to present further evidence of my behaviour, such as asking opening questions in order to get what I want through the estate agents three, who complied by confirming the dungeon will not sell unless it is reduced, and as a result he no longer wants the dungeon to be marketed with estate agent three. The dossier also included a letter from the hospital confirming he understands what is being said to him, but he can't understand what swallowing is – where this plays its part, I have no idea. Two copies of this dossier were sent fourteen days prior to the hearing; one to the court for the attention of the district judge sitting in the hearing and the other to solicitor two. This has completely overthrown solicitor two, whose approach of suck it and see what happens, has just happened – they are having a tantrum, demanding he can't do this to them. He can and he will – being unprepared is their downfall, which he will take complete advantage of. I keep saying they need to be prepared but my information is always irrelevant to solicitor two, and I am the one that will suffer as a result of their continual failings.

Solicitor two doesn't visualise the bigger picture beyond making the application to court. I feel I just pay them to fill the application forms in – it is all they are good for. They are not interested in anything beyond this. They are not interested because it would mean becoming involved – how can you not? Aren't you fighting for your clients rights? Isn't that what being a solicitor is all about?

After being ushered into the courtroom, solicitor two is frantically looking through the pile of paperwork for this dossier that Damian is claiming to have sent to them, with a copy of a certificate of posting to prove this was done, exhibited on page thirteen of the dossier which he drew to the attention of district judge two sitting in the hearing. Solicitor two is more than happy to accept full responsibility for not receiving this dossier in the post, suggesting it may have been lost, and as a result they have not received it. Defending Damian of his actions – which he has done with all intent and purpose – is not helping my case, it is helping him keep repeating this pattern of behaviour that has been ongoing throughout the hearings, and in doing so he gets what he wants, which is to return back to court. He knows full well that this lengthy document with added red herrings and edited documents – he has used black marker pen to cross out words in the statements to the point that they have become unreadable and it looks like a code that needs to be decoded by the military, as there is no way of knowing what it means – will cause more confusion and waste more time.

When questioned by district judge two about this and about his statement for costs relating to his time taken up in preparing these documents for court (which he wouldn't be entitled to any due to not working), he pleaded ignorance and used his disability, claiming it causes him not to understand what has been verbally said to him. Given the lengthy dossier and its contents, there wasn't sufficient time to go through this with it only being allocated a thirty-minute hearing. District judge two had no option – with all the relevant paper work filled in at this stage of the sale – but to adjourn the hearing for a further six weeks, to assess how much time would be needed, if a further hearing is required to discuss the contents of this dossier. However if the sale is completed by this time, the hearing will need to be cancelled.

Damian made his quick exit, walking out of the court room with the notes he made throughout the hearing (exposing his normal handwriting) tucked under his armpit, and his walking stick hanging in the crease of his elbow while his hand holds on tightly to the strap of his bag, preventing it from slipping off his shoulder. Solicitor two is desperately trying to justify to me about this hearing and why it was so necessary. Their explanation is pointless. I am furious with this person failing to listen or believe me or take any notice of what is happening right there in front of them. Why on earth would they ask for costs to cover my time taken off from work to attend court, at such a low level for Damian to pay?

They then inform me that it will not be worth pursuing as it will cost more in court fees, combined with their fees – I will be at a further loss, while Damian's seventy percent remains intact. Solicitor two, having based their entire defence for the scheduled hearing on pre-empting the sale falling through and the dungeon being remarketed at a lower price, given the feedback and amount of viewings, maintains they cannot pre-empt any difficulties that may arise with the sale of the dungeon. They don't have a crystal ball, it is suck it and see.

Guru solicitor can list several difficulties: setting the dungeon on fire, causing internal structural damage, refusing to leave, pretending to need more time to find a property, and delaying the completion date. Yet solicitor two refuses to acknowledge any potential difficulties and can only sympathise with the plight of Damian, whose needs are greater. They have messed up my case, and have been constantly manipulated by Damian, the ex-solicitor proclaiming the disability act, who has proven to them he isn't as disabled as he likes to make out in the court hearings. They have made no attempt to resolve this, only to line their law firm's pockets with further money they can extort from me. Finally, I was in a position with no more estimated costs – I only had to pay solicitor two for the work they have done and any court fees. Unlike the divorce and financial hearings, if you choose to cancel there are penalties, and you have to pay for the work regardless. I was able to sack solicitor two and instruct guru solicitor to be on hand if I needed them, if any difficulties arose with the sale of the house.

The difference was remarkable. Whilst solicitor two issued a final demand for payment or else they won't release my case notes, guru solicitor's correspondence was totally different – professional, polite and courteous in their comments. They were there to help with any difficulties I may encounter, which put me at ease. I knew instantly they would do their utmost to help me, preventing the sale of the dungeon from being lost.

The buyers made contact with me. I asked the estate agent to pass my contact details on to them, so we could update each other where we were at, and if there were any potential problems to try and resolve them. I have waited so long for this moment, knowing eight weeks from now it will be done, and I can finally let go. With the surveyor booked for a month's time, the buyers were more than keen, and had suggested a date for completion – however, they weren't feeling very confident about this happening. They were currently renting, and wanted to know how things were at our end. Trying to be diplomatic – I didn't want to involve them in any of the things that have been happening, but you have to stick to the facts of where you are at, otherwise you are at a greater risk of losing the sale – I could only comment that I had moved out some years ago and that Damian has instructed a conveyancer. I would contact our conveyancer for further information. Most people when they are moving use the same conveyancer when buying another property as it is easier, unlike Damian who has instructed his own conveyancer.

Our joint conveyancer had to contact his conveyancer, but they were instructed by Damian that under no circumstances were they to speak to our joint conveyancer about his purchase without his prior consent. This duty of care, which all conveyancers are bound by, means they cannot disclose any information whatsoever. All the joint conveyancer could do was contact the buyers, and inform them they were waiting for replies to queries, which meant they were waiting for Damian's response to whether he was agreeable to the joint conveyancer being able to talk to his conveyancer about the purchase of his property. The joint conveyancer had no idea whether he had an actual property – not that I care or want to know what stone he decides to live under, I really don't want to know – only is it a genuine yes or no is all I need to know. All the joint conveyancer can do is to take it that he has one, and proceed along as with a normal sale.

I was quietly relieved when the buyers contacted me to inform me that the surveyor wasn't able to get to the dungeon. The weather had been bad with the snow, so this would give us time, with what was frantically happening behind the scenes, which I am desperate to have sorted out so the buyers don't know. Damian finally responded, after numerous letters and emails, but only to confirm the date wasn't suitable. He gave no suggestions of what would be a suitable date for completion, and did not confirm as to whether he was agreeable to the joint conveyancer talking to his conveyancer – there was no way of knowing at what stage he is at with his purchase.

Having to wait another month before the surveyor can go back to the dungeon to do the report, seems a long time to have to wait. Thankfully, this hasn't put the buyers off – they are more than keen with the continual flow of questions they keep asking about the dungeon. It is becoming a bit of a full-time job having the time to respond back to them fairly quickly in between work commitments; it is not always that easy, and they have already requested a further date for completion of the dungeon.

Damian's response to the new completion date is to ignore it and by doing so is causing the buyers to get anxious to the point they are putting pressure on me. Knowing they have the upper hand, they remind me not only have they spent a lot of money to get to this point – one thousand pounds, a fee which every person buying a house will have to pay – but also that they don't want the cost of renting another month. Their plan is to do all the work that needs doing in modernising the dungeon in a month, then move in. If the completion date isn't agreed to, they will have no option but to pull out of the sale, and will be seeking to reclaim these costs they have had to pay, by means of personally suing myself, Damian, and his parents for wasting their time. Guru solicitor wasted no time in contacting the buyers' conveyancer and told them, in no uncertain terms, that they could not do this, as the surveyor had yet to go to the dungeon and they hadn't signed the paperwork in confirming they are definitely buying the dungeon.

Clearly this wasn't what the buyer was expecting, and very quickly contacted myself, blaming their outburst on their busy working schedule. They therefore handed the dealings of their purchase of the dungeon over to their father, who will from now on deal with all aspects, and all communication will be directly through him. He has already been regularly attending the offices of estate agent three, and the conveyancers on behalf of his daughter, and son-in-law to see how the sale is proceeding from the very beginning. He is showing characteristics not that dissimilar to Damian, with limited patience and also continually threatening legal proceedings if their daughter's needs are not fully accommodated. This is causing alarm bells to ring when anyone meets him, and with Damian adding fuel to the fire by rubbing him up the wrong

215

way, which ignites this man further, causing him to explode. His volatile nature becomes more apparent, to the point that everyone involved in the sale of the dungeon is saying he is the problem, and his behaviour is overtaking the silent but deadly Damian's to the degree that estate agent three must have been worn down to the ground with this father's demands. They are refusing to discuss the sale with him, and will only communicate with the buyers, his beloved daughter and son-in-law. Damian's constant refusal to acknowledge any of the emails or letters sent to him by the joint conveyancer makes it all too apparent what he is doing, and even more so that he will still not allow the joint conveyancer to talk to his conveyancer.

Joint conveyancer cannot disclose to anyone, including guru solicitor, which conveyancer is acting on behalf of Damian's purchase. If they were to, they would be in breach of confidentiality and, bound by the duty of care in that they represent both of us with the sale of the dungeon, in no uncertain terms can they discuss about either one of us or pass on any information unless it was ordered by a court that they could.

Guru solicitor notified Damian that, if he fails to continually acknowledge joint conveyancer's correspondence, we would be going to court and drawing this to the district judge's attention. Due to the failure of the postal service to deliver any post to him, he is unaware of any great urgency for a completion date, as the buyers have personally agreed with Damian to take as much time as he wants to in moving out – they are understanding of his disabilities. The fact that he doesn't get out much should not be held against him, or that he has to solely rely on his father taking him out in the car to the library, when he feels well enough, to access a computer so he can read any emails he may have. Damian has ensured all links of communication to him are severed, in order to prevent the joint conveyancer contacting him. There are no lengths he won't go to, including forbidding any contact via his parents, claiming he hasn't the luxury of owning a mobile phone, and with no instructing solicitor representing him to contact him either, he made it more difficult than it should be.

Also he is exposing the web of deceit he continually spins – he insists that his parents are not to be involved, yet they do all the viewings, and estate agent three have confirmed all of these bookings by phoning Damian's mobile phone. Everyone is duty bound not to disclose anything with one another, and he is taking full advantage of this – the sale of the dungeon is constantly held down by this man and we are all totally at his mercy.

Finally the completion date was accepted on the proviso his purchase is ready – his conveyancer confirmed to the joint conveyancer that they were waiting for information to come back, but couldn't elaborate any further on this. However, they could confirm their client has his mortgage in place for his purchase. Are my ears hearing correctly, he has a mortgage? His whole case was built around him being so ill that he needed to live mortgage-free, with being unable to work, and not in a position to get a mortgage whilst living on a pittance with money given to him from the state benefits – this is why he had to have a greater share to be re-housed. How can he get a mortgage with living on state benefits? How much has he got one for, and has he paid a deposit to be able to get this mortgage? There are many questions I want answers to, but I know I am not going to get them. With less than a week to the completion date, the buyers' intensity with communication has increased.

They comment about being informed the sale was going to be quick, and how the surveyors report deeply concerns them with what they have read about the roof, the chimney, and the damp in the basement. There is no direct indication of what they are wanting, other than dumping this information on my lap, and for me to somehow interpret and deal with it. In order to fit the pieces of the puzzle, I have had to contact the joint conveyancer, and estate agent three to figure out what is happening. Do they want the work doing before the completion date, or is it simply they want to negotiate the price of the dungeon, which happens on most purchases whereby the sellers amicably agree to something. Except this isn't a straightforward situation, and unfortunately for this to happen an application would have to be made to the court for a reduction in the price. Waiting for the hearing, which could take a couple of months, would run the risk of possibly losing the sale, since we are already on sticky ground, being three months overdue in completing.

As it transpires, the buyers have not made any further communication in relating to the purchase of the dungeon, and as far as joint conveyancer is concerned it is all going ahead as there is no other reason to think otherwise. All the relevant information regarding Damian's purchase has been received. Estate agent three confirmed that the surveyor's report flagged up a couple of roof tiles need replacing and damp in the cellar – nothing too major, given the condition of the dungeon.

They too hadn't heard anything from the buyers since the report had been done. All of this is more puzzling, even more so as, two days later, the buyers are wanting to go back to the dungeon before finally agreeing to the purchase of the dungeon. They need to take a builder and are desperate to go – with four days to completion, there isn't much time, what with their work commitments. They ask if I have any details for them to contact Damian or his parents. I don't, and if I were to pass his parents' details on, the destruction that would occur as a result would be devastating in that Damian would certainly pull the plug on the sale of the dungeon. There is no way I would jeopardise this – I have waited so long. My mind and body is so desperate to recover from this aftermath it has gone through that it is already starting to let go. The physical symptoms scare me – the trembling in my body and the stiffness in my hands – I can barely openly stretch out my fingers, for the constant ache in my knuckles from having to hold on has taken its toll.

Trying to help the buyers, I contacted estate agent three, who had already been contacted by the buyers, and had tried numerous times to contact Damian with emails and telephone messages left with his parents, as he is not answering his mobile phone, or it is switched off. Damian's failure to respond is creating a fuelled tension for the buyers, and in an desperate attempt to make contact with Damian, they took it upon themselves by firstly hand delivering a letter into the post box at the dungeon.

His lack of response to this caused them to return within ten minutes of delivering this, look inside the post box to see if their letter was still in there. They looked inside the post box to see it had been emptied, which would bring you to the conclusion that Damian is in residence. They decided to climb over the padlocked gates, and to knock at the door, only to be ignored. In a last bid attempt, the buyers tried knocking on the surrounding neighbours' doors to see if they could be of any help. To add further insult, the buyers were informed by a neighbour, who speaks often to Damian, that he has no desire to move, and doesn't want to sell the dungeon – it is all that he has left in the world.

All of this was relayed back by a rather angry father of the buyer to estate agent three, who unfortunately had to bear the brunt of Damian's actions in dealing with a vocal volcano that had erupted in their office. He feels their daughter's time, and money paid into purchasing the dungeon has been wasted on a property that was never intended to be sold, with the threat of legal action being held against the head of estate agent three for their part in all of this. This resulted in the manager of estate agent three not only contacting myself but also Damian to try and resolve this difficult situation, which has got completely out of hand – in order to do so, they need to find out where the problem lies.

It's not rocket science. They can see from their notes how clear my views are about the dungeon – it needs to be sold. If they have not heard anything from Damian by the end of the day, the buyers are to be notified that I will take the day off from work, and go and meet them at the dungeon with their builder. I will open the door so they can go inside the dungeon; could they inform Damian of this? It soon got his attention and he agreed to be there – however, he was concerned for the buyers' health and safety due to the amount of boxes scattered everywhere inside the dungeon, and he wouldn't want them to have an accident.

Then, rather oddly the father of the buyer wanted to contact me for some reason, so I agreed. He was very keen on meeting up for a coffee, to discuss the dungeon saga, saying that Damian has run them ragged, and will I help their daughter buy the dungeon. I didn't think it was appropriate to meet him given the circumstances, so I kept to the facts as guru solicitor advised me to. I was glad his daughter was buying the dungeon, and I understand from the conveyancer all is ready to go ahead, and complete. To which he responded that I am missing the point completely, and further insisting I should meet with him for coffee. He went on, claiming this whole process has torn his beautiful family apart, and they have admitted defeat in purchasing the dungeon. With no notification from the buyers, neither the joint conveyancer, or the estate agent three were aware the buyers were admitting defeat in purchasing the dungeon.

Estate agent three was refusing to deal with the father of the buyer, claiming he was mental and verbally abusive towards staff, so they would only deal directly with the buyers – his daughter and son-in-law. I tried to find out from the buyers themselves what is really happening, only to receive a response from the father of the buyer, which was not what I was expecting. A brief message written "Looks like I will be buying you a coffee at the courthouse" and enclosed an email attachment to open. The attachment listed reasons why they have pulled out of the purchase of the dungeon, naming those who are responsible – Damian, both of his parents, myself and the manager of estate agent three – and the reasons why each one of us are to be held responsible, as it is our actions that have caused this to occur. He highlighted that it is mine, and Damian's parents', fault that the entire responsibility has fallen upon Damian, who is too severely ill to move out, let alone sell the dungeon, and given how stressful it is he shouldn't be doing this, and if we had all communicated more this wouldn't have happened. He cited our failure to respond to the events that occurred in trying to further review the dungeon with their builder, and the loss of earnings – as a result, they are going to personally sue us. I can't believe this is happening. Is this definite? I need to know from the buyers directly but they have gone into hiding. I have left messages asking them to contact the estate agent three as they have been trying to get a hold of them to know what the situation is, and can they confirm whether or not they are buying the dungeon as we need to know.

They claim they did inform the estate agent three that they had withdrawn their offer, while estate agent three still maintains they had no knowledge of this. I really don't know what to believe any more – my head is spinning, and I am back to holding on to the cliff. I don't honestly know if I can do this any more. I am so exhausted having to continually keep pushing any obstacles Damian keeps putting in the way.

Always constantly at his mercy estate agent three is waiting for Damian's approval to continue marketing the dungeon. Regardless of the fact that I have given them the go-ahead to re-market it, they still have to wait for his approval. They didn't wait for my instructions when he instructed them, so what's the difference, other than I am a female and he is a man.

They already have his approval on the piece of paper he signed agreeing to their terms and conditions in marketing the dungeon. There is no need for this delay, the longer the dungeon is off the market the longer it is going to sell. Five months have been wasted, and we are still no nearer to getting the dungeon sold, but estate agent three reassures me they will do their utmost in selling the dungeon. Was I aware there was no for-sale board up? They had noticed it was missing a few weeks ago when viewing another property. No one thought to mention this to me, blaming it on the windy weather or children stealing the board. These are the only reasons, not the man that lives there could have possibly ordered his father to take it down.

Thankfully guru solicitor is on the case, and wasted no time in contacting the courts regarding the loss of the sale – our differences are all too apparent, and as a result this has occurred. With what happened at the last hearing with solicitor two being given a file bundle from Damian only minutes before the hearing, guru solicitor needs to be aware of what to possibly expect. They suggested we meet before the hearing to prepare, and plan a strategy to cover all possible eventualities that Damian may throw at the hearing.

The worst possible event that could happen to a solicitor did unfortunately happen to guru solicitor, being unable to speak due to having an accident, which meant guru solicitor would not be able to represent me at the court hearing. With forty-eight hours to go, a locum with a very firm handshake took over my case and had very little time to get up to speed with my case. Which, remarkably, they did, like a whirlwind who spoke faster than a high-speed train and had a plan for every possible argument that may be thrown at us. Fate works in mysterious ways – whirlwind locum solicitor just so happens to work at the very law firm that Damian has instructed to act on behalf of his purchase of his sizeable property – you would need a considerable amount of money, as well as the seventy percent of the dungeon, to be in a position to purchase it. Whirlwind locum solicitor decided in our defence, although it was a risky one, to ask the vocal volcano – the father of the buyer, the very one who is threatening legal action against me – to help strengthen my case.

They suggested that we ask him to be a witness, and possibly to testify in court, by giving a statement of their version of accounts that occurred during the process of attempting to buy the dungeon. The events, which I thought they knew nothing about, to my horror they did, and more was revealed during the statement taken down by the locum solicitor. On the very day the surveyor was due to do the report on the dungeon, they were contacted by Damian, who cancelled the survey being done, and made them wait a month before they would be allowed to come back to do the report for the buyers. There were certain jobs that needed doing in the dungeon and they were informed they would be done. They never were. They had to wait weeks for a viewing and, when they did eventually go, they were made to feel very unwelcome during the viewings, and in particular during the second one when they were greeted with "it's not you again." All of this has fuelled an angry father of the buyer to launch their own personal investigation into the sale history of the dungeon, and, in doing so, has uncovered that each of the previous estate agents are also vying for Damian's blood for the way he has treated them. Damian has even taken the dungeon off the market – I found out purely by chance when I went on the estate agent three's website to see that this property has been withdrawn from the open market. He was ignoring estate agent three's messages – they had a waiting list of people wanting to go for a viewing and Damian apparently claimed I had instructed two other estate agents to market the dungeon. Based on this information, estate agent three decided after this to withdraw from marketing the dungeon. Damian had got what he wanted.

The sun was shining as I walked up to the court building with my sunglasses on, and a splash of red lipstick, newspaper in one hand, and a takeaway coffee in the other hand. I stood there and paused to take a drink of coffee and bask in the glory of the sun, before casually entering the court building, all performed in full view of Damian's father standing across the road. He was on look-out duty and would report back to Damian, who was sitting waiting in the car, what he had just witnessed. While I waited in the court waiting area for locum solicitor to arrive, I continued drinking the coffee I had bought, and reading the newspaper, appearing not to care that I was there, and, more importantly, not to care or even to notice Damian had walked past me. Whirlwind locum solicitor ushered me into a private waiting room for a further discussion before we entered the courtroom. As it was a directional hearing, it was only listed for thirty minutes so we may not be able to discuss everything that we want to say, so not to be too disappointed. They have narrowed it down to focus on the most important part – Damian's blatant sabotage throughout the sale and that the dungeon needs to be reduced further, as there is six months further deprivation to be considered. All depends on what the district judge decides to order; there is no way of knowing. Damian's new solicitor is under his influence, and totally enthralled by him, declaring to whirlwind locum solicitor that their client has done no wrong, and has yet to hear anything bad said of their moral law abiding client.

Whirlwind locum solicitor produced the email I was sent from estate agent three, revealing what his client had done in withdrawing the dungeon from the open market, to which a very quiet solicitor quickly left the corridor, no doubt heading in the direction towards their client.

District judge three is sitting in the hearing and is in a foul mood, tugging at the papers piled in front of them trying to make sense of the submitted documents, some of which Damian has personally submitted to the court. They demand to know what this is about? Referring to the piles of paper.

Whirlwind locum solicitor goes first, to which Damian's solicitor responds and refers to their client as their "learned friend" while I am referred to as "She," the cat's mother. All of this further exasperates district judge three, who insists this is simplified to what it boils down to. When the word valuation is mentioned by whirlwind locum solicitor, district judge three erupts further at this pettiness, questioning why this can't be agreed out of court and promptly accuses the solicitors of increasing the costs – not that the court have had any part in any of the excessive court hearings! We will no doubt end up having another hearing, as district judge three is requesting a two-page document from each of our solicitors to state our case in relation to the sale of the dungeon. The outcome of this will be greatly affected by the results of the valuation that is to take place, and organised by no other than Damian, who has been further reprimanded in court for his continual actions in sending lengthy documents to court. He has been ordered to stop, but he won't – he will continue in what he is doing.

The hearing is dismissed and the strain of it has been too much for Damian who storms out. Whirlwind locum solicitor does not want Damian influencing the estate agent, like he has previously done with the pricing, and has set out writing a letter, including adding part of the 'red book'. This is a guide on how to value – it sets the legal requirements that estate agents should adhere to. This is the last I will see of whirlwind locum solicitor, who has made an important step forward in resolving my case – they attempted to help fight my case.

Because of what I did in the courtroom, the first time I have been able to do this – I actually sat directly across from Damian and faced him in the courtroom, he felt the need to remind me who is in charge. I need to be punished for my actions, and for this he reported me to the police with a fabricated story. What it is, I don't know – only that when the police logged this, they saw the number of incidents relating to Damian, and this alerted them to contact me. They were concerned for my safety and advised me that I should contact my solicitor immediately, and get a non-molestation order made against him as soon as possible. As I simply can't afford one, they alternatively suggested I do it myself; there would be costs but they would be lower. They would send me a leaflet about this, offered me free counselling, and advised me to keep reporting all incidents to help them with the picture they need to build up – an image of what is happening and, in the event of anything happening, dial 999.

With this information, they have dumped their responsibility yet again on my lap, but what am I supposed to do with this? I have no power in the law. You have to go to the authority that deals with this, that is the police, and what do I say? The police are really concerned about my safety, so much so that they have phoned me to warn me that I am at risk, but won't do anything about it. It is not acceptable to keep doing this to me – warning me and doing nothing. Either do something or don't – by doing this, they are maintaining Damian's emotional and psychological abuse against me, and in doing so they are aiding and abetting him to continue with the mental torture. I did as I was advised by the police officer, and after having re-discussed the costs of obtaining a non-molestation order – fees at one thousand and five hundred pounds will only get two court hearings to plead your case – and if Damian were to contest the non-molestation order, then further fees would apply. Based on past events, it would be more likely in the region of five thousand pounds, which I simply don't have. Locum two solicitor advised the only other option, was to make a formal written complaint about the police.

This resulted in three phone calls from the police. One assessed if their police officers at the station were to be held responsible, another one also assessed if they were accountable, asking if the police officer was rude when they informed me that I was at risk. In their opinion, they thought it was very considerate of the officer to do this, as they weren't obliged to do so, and they implied that I was being ungrateful for what the courteous caring actions of this officer had done for me. The third was from a liaison officer, working closely with the police acting as the go-between, trying to help resolve matters by reporting back to them my grievance. All they can do is try to pacify me, claiming that my case will be dealt with differently this time. Giving me the same old trash I have repeatedly heard time after time: keep reporting all incidents to the police, they need to build a picture of what is happening, do I feel threatened, do I feel scared, dial 999 if you see him, and run. Then they suggested going over safety procedures again with me to see if I have them all in place and, when I heard this, I lost the will to live – I would rather watch paint dry, because it is more productive and you get the finished result.

District judge three's actions of having a bad day cost me three thousand pounds, and I was back to square one, in that I have to repeat the whole process again of gathering evidence of Damian trying to prevent selling the dungeon. Despite the dungeon being marketed with three different estate agents in two years, and numerous viewings, delaying viewings by ignoring the estate agents' messages, limiting to when viewers can attend, in precise two hour time frames, strictly no midweek viewings, cancelling a surveyor and an ex-buyer that is threatening legal proceedings for his actions – how much more evidence do you possibly need? I have to do this all over again with another estate agent, unable to go back to the court with any difficulties, as district judge three stipulated in their court order, that the earliest this can be reviewed back at the court is in one year's time.

All guru solicitor can do is shrug their shoulders at this and give me their bill. That's it? Nothing more can be done, no action plan. Their parting words of advice is that it requires on my part, effort and hard work in gathering evidence – I need to keep on top of the estate agents with what is happening on a weekly basis and using the law to win this. From this very moment I felt guru solicitor had already turned their back on helping me, and had already closed the door on my case firmly shut, for it to be shelved and left to gather dust.

I am no further forward, only greater in debt, with worsening health and having to relive this whole cycle again. Knowing what I know now, it would have been easier to sign the dungeon over to the court so the district judges, and solicitors can fight amongst themselves who gets what from the money pot. There is only one winner in the law – that's the law.

Beggar's Belief

Something has to change. It's pointless going back to court – been there, done that, so many times that I already know what the outcome will be – a waste of time and more money that I don't have. Contacting guru solicitor is out of the question; since their readiness to shelve my case, I have lost my faith in them.

My other option is to contact another local MP (member of parliament) and plead my case face to face about what has been happening. I have nowhere else to go. I need help and, as my local MP, they are there to listen, and help with people living in there constituency with any problems that they may have. I set out in a detailed dossier, in chronological order, what has been happening in the last five years with the police lack of involvement, and all of the district judges at the county court. It didn't take long for this sympathetic MP to grasp the full situation, and understand the fullness of this and how I felt that my human rights are continually being constrained in getting help, for no one is prepared to resolve this dire situation that goes on and on. While Damian exercises his right to continue to emotionally and psychologically abuse me by using his legal knowledge, manipulating the police and district judges they too have become actively involved in the ongoing abuse.

Offering assistance to my plight, the MP's office contacted guru solicitor, asking what can they do to help, only to be informed their assistance isn't required.

My heart sank when I heard the voice on my voicemail, another police officer leaving their contact number for me to phone them back. I can honestly say it wasn't what I was expecting to hear when I spoke to them. This police officer wasn't concerned for my safety but for Damian's, which required me to be questioned by them at the police station where they worked. I tried explaining to the police officer that this was all about Damian maintaining the level of emotional and psychological abuse, using his knowledge of the law, what with being a former solicitor, and involving the police to actively do this for him. This police officer dismissed this, refusing to accept that it was relevant to the case, and if I didn't go to the police station for questioning they would come, and if necessary forcibly arrest me. This police officer is the worse one by far I have encountered, for they had already decided in their mind immediately after talking to Damian that I was guilty of harassing him, and all that remained was getting me convicted for this crime I haven't done.

They informed me of my rights and also their rights – I am allowed to have legal representation whilst being questioned, and afterwards they require my fingerprints, DNA and a sample of my handwriting for evidence. I cannot believe what this police officer is doing, and, even more disturbing, in order to obtain my contact telephone number, they would have had to gone through the police-reported incidents they have logged regarding Damian, and this is worrying.

I sat anxiously waiting on the toughened plastic bench bolted into the floor inside the police station. Whilst the legal representative – I have had to instruct one who specializes in criminal law – is discussing in a paper-thin walled room behind the closed door, with the investigating police officer, the written information I have given them detailing the history of events, and about the police being manipulated into assisting Damian with the emotional and psychological abuse. I can hear everything this police officer is saying, denying any knowledge of this and rebuking this as nonsense – the questioning was going ahead.

Before being questioned I was allowed discussion time with the criminal solicitor, who asked had I ever been a suspect before. Due to this being my first time, they explained what will happen during the questioning – it will be recorded on a CD which will be then produced in a court of law and used as evidence against you for the court to decide what your sentence will be. I will be cautioned on the recording, and asked to confirm my name, date of birth and address and that I understand I am to be questioned. You have the right to leave at any point during the questioning, but actually you don't and, if you do, you will be arrested. Afterwards I will be taken through to the cell area for fingerprinting and a DNA sample. They asked if I am aware of the charges against me in relation to the harassment of Damian.

I have no idea, all I know he is putting pressure on me by using the police. Damian has reported I have sent him, in over two months, ten notes with messages on; which were all hand delivered and posted at the dungeon.

The criminal solicitor couldn't go too much into detail about what was written on these notes, other than they were the size of five centimetres by five centimetres with two or three words on them. They needed to see a sample of my handwriting and asked me to write down certain words. After looking at my handwriting, they immediately informed me it doesn't look good for me, as my handwriting matches the ones on the notes and, with Damian being a fragile man, "you're screwed." Can I explain how my fingerprints have ended up on these notes? I haven't even been finger printed, and already they are talking about what conviction I could likely get. There are many documents I have had to sign relating to the legal proceedings with the divorce, and financial settlement, and more recently with the conveyancer; all have my signatures and are covered in my fingerprints. I am advised to mention this when being questioned, as it may help in my defence even if they don't believe me.

Before I am questioned by the police officer they briefly had a private conversation with the criminal solicitor, who returns to relay the message that is to be passed on to me.

I am only to answer the questions that are asked of me, I am not allowed to talk about the domestic abuse as we will be there all night – is that understood? Sat in the small interview room with the police officer out for my blood and a second police officer to assist if necessary in the questioning and the criminal solicitor, it brought back the memories of when I tried to escape from the dungeon – he said no one would believe me and there was no one there to help me. How vulnerable do I feel in that interview room.

Words fail me. How can I do this and not talk about the abuse because this is what it all relates to? How can I defend myself if I am not supposed to talk about it? The exhibits were shown to me in sealed bags, these ten notes with messages on them that barely make up a paragraph. Damian had taken the time to wade through many of the written letters he had kept from our relationship, and cut out random words to place myself directly in the frame, signed yours truly. Also added a few of his own, to cause further stress, by adding an emblem relating to a paedophile, to remind me of my own child abuse, and one sexual one relating to my love, and a few rusty scalpel blades he emptied from the sharps bin to add greater impact. The police officer demanded an explanation to what each of these messages meant, but how would I know? I didn't send them. All I know is that I am not allowed to say that it is a direct message and a threat to myself of what he intends to do, and this police officer who feels it is their duty, to what I can only say is horrendous in what they are subjecting me to, as well as delivering Damian's mail, is continuing with emotional and psychological abuse.

To prolong the torture further – after an exhausting three hours – I was informed it doesn't end here today by the criminal solicitor. If I am invited back to the station for an interview in possibly two to three months' time then I will need to contact them, as they will attend this interview with me, and also represent myself during the court hearing. The best you can hope is that they never contact you, as it means no charges are to be brought against you.

It beggars belief what's happening and even more so that the following day I am standing inside another police station reporting the police to the police, and relaying the full details that have occurred. Having never been a suspect in my life, how would I know I should have had someone there from PPU or the domestic abuse organization – I was never given the opportunity by the police officer.

Further discussions in relaying over again what has happened to PPU, who are questioning this – it should have never taken place. Other factors should have been taken into account, such as the length of time of the relationship – I was with Damian for eighteen years, so my fingerprints will be on everything, and once they are on something, unless they are cleaned off they are on there for life. This police officer would have been aware of the history when they retrieved my phone number from the police records – for them to deny any of this is unacceptable, when it's clearly emotional and psychological abuse. PPU suggested I was within my rights to make a formal complaint about this police officer.

However, their actions were backed by their boss – this police officer is an outstanding and dedicated member of the team, and they will not be taken off this investigation, their role is not to find you guilty but to prove your innocence. Clearly not, as in my case this police officer decided from the very beginning to ignore the history and proceed, as I am an easy conviction.

I then had to relay all of what has happened to guru solicitor to keep them updated of the situation. No doubt Damian will be using this to prevent me from doing any viewings at the dungeon. He is too ill for anyone to come, and an accompanied viewing by the estate agent is out of the question at this time – he can't say when the time will be. What other alternative is there, when a desperate estate agent four contacts you explaining the difficult position they are in with a waiting list of people wanting to view the dungeon.

With a free review into my case, guru solicitor is no longer shrugging their shoulders; they are ready to spring into action and would be delighted to win my case. What's brought this on? It may possibly have something to do with myself going directly to the MP, for what I am doing would be exposing the actions of the legal system, including the role of solicitor two (who by all accounts, according to guru, is a very good solicitor).

By refusing the help of the MP, this would defuse the situation and stop it dead in its tracks, knowing the MP cannot proceed in where I want my case to be brought to – one of the ministers of justice.

Highlighting that an MP cannot help my case, only to be there to sympathize, and with this guru solicitor made every effort to try to restore my faith in them. They devised an action plan worthy of military award, about what I do if I am asked to return back to the police station for an interview. Don't give in to the pressure of the police officer – they have their own targets to meet on how many convictions they get in a month at the police station. Refuse a cautionary warning, because this means you accept full responsibility, and it means you have been charged at the police station rather than being charged at the court, and you will have a record. We may have to go back to court about the dungeon, and on and on it goes and at the same time shielding their friend from the line of fire, so I don't pursue my case any further than the four walls of the county court or the four walls I am sitting in.

I then relay what has happened to each of three domestic abuse organisations, in my desperate attempt for someone to help me. Only to be informed I either don't meet their criteria for them to help me, or there is nothing more that can be done, because I have done all the suggestions and been down all the routes I have been advised to take, more than once, and exhausted them all.

No one can do anything, all I am offered is emotional support, tea and biscuits to help me deal with this. I am far too practical, knowing this isn't going to alter my situation. Emotional support isn't helping me to stop the police in what they are doing, or make the district judges see sense or stop the chief super intendent who continually ignores my formal complaint, and has made no effort into bringing a resolution to this, no matter how I have tried, or stopped my desperate plea for help from one of the ministers of justice from falling into the abyss.

So my fight for my right to be continues. I will be listened to and believed. It is unacceptable that I am expected to have to live my life like this. I shouldn't have to live a life in constant fear. I just have to find the right person and I aim to do so.

TODAY I AM GOING TO BE MAGNIFICENT

What has been the worst part of my life – I can only describe as mental and physical hell on earth – has also turned out to be the start of new beginnings and these have brought something into my life that I have always longed to feel, and that is happiness. Alongside other emotions I am experiencing, I am learning to accept it is OK to feel like this, and by embracing them it has given me the freedom to open up, and express my feelings, which hasn't been easy. For me, I needed to know who I am, and the only way of doing this was to explore my past from my childhood right through to present day. Through doing this, by having counselling, the pieces form a picture that made sense of the puzzle. There is no doubt that the relationship I had with my parents had made such an imprint on my personality that it was inevitable I would up end up having an unhealthy relationship with someone who had similar traits – they would treat me in the way I have become accustomed to, and only ever known. With most of the work having been done, the foundations had already been installed inside me for someone who is prepared to carry on maintaining the level of guilt that my father had installed when I was seven years of age. Along with the emotional, and psychological demands like my mother placed upon me, for the consequences I would face if I ever upset her, which meant life with her was practically being an invisible daughter who was never allowed to voice opinions or express any emotions, as she could not handle this.

All of this, along with her constant need for attention, and hunger to be entertained – if not, the constant threats of suicide were placed in front of me to somehow deal with – led me to walk out of one fire and into the blaze of another. Damian's fire is burning with a very similar flame, except there is a difference which probably drew me to it – the obsession he had about me that was growing into an unhealthy fixation. I accepted this as a sign of being caring – someone for the first time in my life was taking an interest in what I did, being the constant centre of his attention – I thought this was an indication of love. Except it wasn't, all that has ever mattered to my parents, and to Damian is maintaining the level of control over me in a bid to keep me hidden, so I remain where they feel I belong: with them to do as they feel necessary. I am just an emotional punch bag, there to be used and abused for their own gratification. The glory of overpowering someone for their own needs becomes a drug for them – this constant craving for power is almost like an elixir to suppress their own insecurities. The thought of what you might grow into, and achieve something, scares them – for you reaching your potential would mean they would lose their power, and they would be left with nothing, only their pitiful world that they exist in.

Having this knowledge and understanding highlighted that I needed to make changes to my own behavioural pattern.

I vowed to myself after I had made my escape from the dungeon that my life has to be better than what it was, by embracing the changes that I have been desperately wanting to do, but dare not, mainly because of the guilt I have carried around with me. If I were a better person, things wouldn't have happened. I blamed myself for everything that went wrong. I hated myself. I understand why I have felt guilty, that it all stemmed from my father's actions when he crossed the boundaries. No father should ever do that to their child and, alongside my mother's and, later, Damian's actions, understanding this allowed me to let go of the guilt. By doing this, and no longer having to be attending to everyone's constant demands that they make of me in order so that I please them, it is now gone. I don't have to do that anymore or seek anyone's approval for the choices I make in my life – the only person I am responsible for in making them happy is myself. The options, and endless choices I now have in my possession is exhilarating. I can stay out as long as I like, come home at whatever time I choose, eat whatever I want, stay in bed, and sleep all day, leave the dirty dishes in the sink, not brush my hair, dance around the kitchen in my pyjamas, make my own decisions, have my own thoughts, and voice my own opinions. This has given me the freedom to explore who I am, the courage to be myself, and for the first time in my life, I have come to love and accept myself.

I am a work in progress – the tools I have to make the changes aren't always that shiny, and that's OK. I am not meant to be perfect; I will make mistakes but I can learn from them, so that my future may take a different direction and history doesn't repeat itself.

This has enabled me to form new friendships and a healthy loving relationship with a truly wonderful person, the love of my life, who makes me happy. They have held my hand tightly to face the storms, kissed the rolling tears from my cheeks, caught me in their arms to protect me from the fall, and loved me back to life. I never knew it was possible to feel so loved, it is all down to this one incredible person that makes me feel the way I do about them. Being in the right relationship, where you can be who you truly are, able to express yourself in all your weird and wonderfulness that you possess. That someone is madly in love with you, embraces all that you are and all that you have yet to become, who loves being with you who respects you, and your body.

It isn't caring when someone demands your silence or prevents you from growing, which requires certain conditions that only apply to you, makes you feel guilty worthless or less of a person than you should be, manipulates or uses whatever force to make you do things against your will, and takes away your freedom, and any choices you may want to make.

It isn't loving to keep you afraid, and fearful, and inflict as much pain as they possibly can to punish you for all the things that have ever gone wrong in their lives – the missed opportunities, the arguments, and fights they have lost, the list is endless and someone has to pay for all the suffering it has caused them – and that someone is you because they feel you deserve it.

Love would want to hear you speak, enjoy the sound of your laughter, and see you smile. It would love you to be all that you can be in this life, and that is to be magnificent you.